Anne of Green Gables

Written By: L.M. Montgomery

Teacher Guide

Published by: Memoria Press
www.memoriapress.com

ISBN: 978-1-61538-069-5

Contributing Editors: Tanya Charlton and Sean Brooks
Cover Illustration by Starr Steinbach
Cover & Layout Design by Karah J. Force

PREPARING TO READ:

REVIEW

- Orally review any previous vocabulary.
- Review the plot of the book as read so far.
- Periodically review the concepts of character, setting, and plot.

STUDY GUIDE PREVIEW

- Reading Notes:
  - Read aloud together
  - This section gives the student key characters, places, terms that are relevant to a particular time period, etc.
- Vocabulary:
  - Read aloud together so that students will recognize words when they come across them in their reading.
- Comprehension Questions:
  - Read through these questions with students to encourage purposeful reading.

READING:

- Student reads the chapter (or selection of the chapter for that lesson) independently or to the teacher (for younger students).
- For younger students, you can alternate between teacher-read and student-read passages. Model good reading skills. Encourage students to read expressively and smoothly. Teacher may occasionally take oral reading grades.
- While reading, mark each vocabulary word as you come across it.
- Have students take note in their study guide margin of pages where a comprehension question is answered.

AFTER READING:

VOCABULARY

- Look at each word within the context that it is used, and help your student come up with the best synonym that defines the word. (Make sure it is a synonym the student knows the meaning of.)
- Record the word's meaning in the students' study guides. (Use students' knowledge of Latin and other vocabulary to decipher meanings.)

COMPREHENSION QUESTIONS

- Older students can answer these questions independently, but younger students (2nd-4th) need to answer the questions orally, form a good sentence, and then write it down, using correct punctuation, capitalization, and spelling. (You may want to write the sentence down for the younger student after forming it orally, and then let the student copy it perfectly.)
- It is not necessary to write the answer to every question. Some may be better answered orally.
- Answering questions and composing answers is a valuable learning activity. Questions require students to think; writing a concise answer is a good composition exercise.

QUOTATIONS AND DISCUSSION QUESTIONS

- Use the Quotations and Discussion Questions section of each lesson as a guide to your oral discussion of the key concepts in the chapter that may not be covered in the comprehension questions.
- These talking points can take your oral discussion to a higher level than covered in the students' written work. Use this time as an opportunity to introduce higher-level thinking. You can introduce concepts the students may not be mature enough to fully understand yet but that would be beneficial for them to begin thinking about.
- A key to the Discussion Questions is in the back of the Teacher Guide.

ENRICHMENT

- The Enrichment activities include composition, copywork, dictation, research, mapping, drawing, poetry work, literary terms, and more.
- This section has a variety of activities in it, but the most valuable activity is composition. Your student should complete at least one composition assignment each week. Proof student's work and have student copy composition until grammatically perfect. Insist on clear, concise writing. For younger students, start with 2-3 sentences, and do the assignment together. The student can form good sentences orally as you write them down, and then the student copies them.
- These activities can be completed as time and interest allow. Do not feel you need to complete all of these activities. Choose the ones that you feel are the best use of your students' time.

UNIT REVIEW AND TESTS

- There is a unit review and a quiz or test following every few lessons (varies by individual guide).
- On the weeks that have these reviews and tests, you may want to do the review early in the week, and then drill it orally a couple of times before giving the test at the end of the week.
- A final comprehensive test is also included.

Contents

Anne of Green Gables

Appendix

Tests

Reading Notes

*Vocabulary words with an asterisk are Mastery Words and will appear in the quizzes.

Avonlea	the town in which most of the story takes place
Mrs. Rachel Lynde	the town gossip; lives next door to the Cuthberts
Marilla Cuthbert	unmarried woman; tall and thin; stern
Matthew Cuthbert	Marilla's unmarried brother; shy
Green Gables	the Cuthberts' home, founded by Matthew and Marilla's father
asylum	a place offering protection and safety; a shelter

Vocabulary

Write the meaning of each bold word or phrase.

1. without due regard for decency and **decorum**. ______ n. polite behavior
2. she had **ferreted** out the whys and wherefores thereof. ______ v. uncovered; hunted out
3. run the unseen **gauntlet** of Mrs. Rachel's all-seeing eye. ______ n. attack from all sides
4. **deftly*** putting this and that together ______ adv. skillfully
5. instead of being an unheard-of **innovation**. ______ n. new idea or method
6. I've had some **qualms** myself. ______ n. uneasy sense of doubt, concerns

*Look up "deft" in the dictionary, and write out the complete definition, the alternate forms, and 2-3 synonyms. *deft:* adj. neatly skillful or dexterous, adroit

alternate forms: deftly - adv. deftness - n.

synonyms: dexterous, skillful, proficient, nimble, astute

Expressions for Discussion

1. *"Well, Marilla, I'll just tell you plain that I think you're doing a mighty foolish thing—a risky thing, that's what."* - Mrs. Lynde What is the foolish thing Marilla is doing? *adopting a child*
2. *"And as for the risk, there's risks in pretty near everything a body does in this world."* - Marilla
3. *"Only don't say I didn't warn you if he burns Green Gables down or puts strychnine in the well—"* - Mrs. Lynde Who is going to burn Green Gables down? *the adopted child*

*Comprehension Question answers with an asterisk indicate important plot points that will appear in the quizzes.

Comprehension Questions

Answer the following in complete sentences.

1. What is the setting and time of this book? (The time is not specified, but we can assume it was written as a modern novel, so use the copyright date.) The setting of this book is Nova Scotia, in Canada. The book was published in 1908, so it is set at the turn of the Twentieth Century.

2. The author does not make the relationship between Matthew and Marilla clear in the beginning of the book. What is their relationship? Matthew and Marilla are brother and sister. This is hinted at when Rachel Lynde says, "Matthew and Marilla were grown up when the new house was built …" Their relationship becomes clear in later chapters.

3. What is Rachel Lynde's surprise? Rachel Lynde's surprise is that Matthew and Marilla are going to adopt a child from an orphanage.

4. What are the requirements Marilla has for the type of child she and Matthew are willing to adopt? The requirements for the adopted child are that it has to be a boy to help Matthew farm, he has to be a native-born Canadian, and he has to be ten or eleven years old.

5. Why does Rachel Lynde not wait at Marilla's house to see the arrival of the new child? Rachel Lynde prefers to visit the neighbors and spread the news rather than wait for Matthew to return because "Mrs. Rachel dearly loved to make a sensation."

6. We are given a good glimpse into the characters of Marilla and Rachel Lynde in this chapter. Name some of their character attributes. Marilla keeps a very neat house and yard, takes the world seriously, is a woman of "narrow experience and rigid conscience," tends toward a sense of humor, and is perceptive of people (as shown in her dealings with Rachel). Rachel Lynde is nosy, a good housewife, a manager of people, devoted to church work, strongly opinionated, observant, outspoken, and a gossip.

Enrichment

1. Locate on a map: Prince Edward Island, Canada

2. Research the following expressions and explain them:

   a. *"A body can get used to anything, even to being hanged."* This is an old proverb with an unknown source. Rachel Lynde's comparison of being hanged to Matthew and Marilla living off of the road is humorous.

   b. *"… the proverbial peck of dirt."* This is another old proverb originating from the idea that one must eat a peck of dirt before one dies.

   c. *"Job's comforting"* When Job was afflicted with tragedy after tragedy, his friends "comforted" him with a list of his shortcomings and a criticism of his anger and disillusionment. This was no comfort to Job, but only made his lot harder to bear. Real comfort would have been sympathetic, not judgmental.

Reading Notes

Bright River	the town where Matthew goes to meet the orphan boy at the train station
Anne Shirley	the story's protagonist; an orphan with red hair and freckles; full of spirit
Mrs. Spencer	a worker at the orphan asylum who brings Anne to the Cuthberts

Vocabulary

Write the meaning of each bold word or phrase.

1. the big eyes were full of spirit and **vivacity***. n. liveliness, animation
2. our **discerning** extraordinary observer adj. showing good judgment or insight
3. of whom shy Matthew Cuthbert was so **ludicrously** afraid. adv. in an absurd or ridiculous manner
4. But there is so little **scope** for the imagination n. range, extent of room
5. She came out of her **reverie** n. daydream
6. spiritual shadings of crocus and rose and **ethereal** green adj. airy, delicate, heavenly

*Look up "vivacious" in the dictionary, and write out the complete definition, the alternate forms, and 2-3 synonyms. *vivacious:* adj. lively; sprightly; animated
alternate forms: vivaciously - adv. vivaciousness - n. vivacity - n.
synonyms: lively, spirited, energetic, spry

Expressions for Discussion

1. *"I've never belonged to anybody—not really."* - Anne
2. *"I do love to imagine I'm nice and plump, with dimples in my elbows."* - Anne
3. *"But am I talking too much? People are always telling me I do. Would you rather I didn't talk? If you say so, I'll stop. I can stop when I make up my mind to, although it's difficult."* - Anne
   Who is Anne talking to? *Matthew*
4. *"Now you see why I can't be perfectly happy. Nobody could who had red hair ... It will be my lifelong sorrow."* - Anne
5. *"Have you ever imagined what it must feel like to be divinely beautiful?"* - Anne
6. *"Well now, I dunno."* - Matthew
7. *When he thought of that rapt light being quenched in her eyes he had an uncomfortable feeling that he was going to assist at murdering something ...* - Matthew
   What is going to quench the light out of Anne's eyes? *finding out that she can't live at Green Gables*
   What does Matthew compare his feelings to? *having to kill a lamb, calf, or any other innocent creature*

Comprehension Questions

Answer the following in complete sentences.

1. Why does Anne want to sit outside the train station instead of inside? There was more "scope for imagination" outside because of the vast countryside. It wasn't nearly as limiting as the inside of a train station. Anne was putting her imagination to good use as she imagined the things that could have prevented Matthew's coming to get her and made plans for spending the night in a cherry tree, imagining she was "dwelling in marble halls."

2. Of what is Matthew afraid? Why? Matthew is afraid of women because he thinks they are secretly laughing at him.

3. What is Anne's only hope of being a bride? Why? Anne's only hope of being a bride is if she can marry a foreign missionary. She thinks she is homely, but a foreign missionary wouldn't be very particular about the looks of his wife.

4. How long was Anne in the orphan asylum? How has she coped with her difficult life up to this point? Anne was in the asylum for four months. She coped with her difficult life by using her imagination, pretending her life was different than it really was.

5. What troubles Matthew as they approach Green Gables? Of whom is he thinking? What does this tell you about his character? Matthew is troubled because he has become sympathetic to Anne and knows she is going to be heartbroken when she finds out she can't live at Green Gables. Matthew is thinking about Anne and her feelings. Matthew is a compassionate, feeling person who puts others ahead of himself.
See Expression #7 on previous page for further discussion.

6. Describe Anne. Name some things that are important to her. Anne is full of life and spirit. She remains cheerful and optimistic even though she has had a difficult life. She has a vivid imagination that she puts to good use. She is polite and thoughtful to Matthew, putting him at ease. She has an appreciation for nature. Physically, Anne is skinny, has red hair, freckles, a pointed chin, and big eyes.

Enrichment

1. Locate on a map: Nova Scotia, Canada

" ... Anne is such an unromantic name."

Reading Notes

White Way of Delight	Anne's name for the "Avenue," a stretch of road where apple trees with white flowers bloom overhead
Lake of Shining Waters	Anne's name for Barry's Pond, a long and winding body of water with many shifting colors in it

Vocabulary

Write the meaning of each bold word or phrase.

1. Marilla and Matthew looked at each other **deprecatingly*** adv. with disapproval
2. "Oh," she added **reproachfully** adv. disapprovingly, rebukingly
3. that's one **consolation**. n. comfort in time of grief
4. and a certain **tempestuous*** appearance of the bed adj. wild; unruly
5. a sure sign of **perturbation** of mind. n. a cause of disturbance or agitation
6. expressed a **predilection** for standing on his head. n. a preference or special liking

*Look up the following words in the dictionary, and write out the complete definition, the alternate forms, and 2-3 synonyms for each word.

deprecate: v. 1. to express disapproval of or a wish against; deplore 2. to plead earnestly against 3. to pray against *alt. forms:* deprecatingly - adv. deprecation - n. deprecative - adj. deprecator - n. deprecatory - adj. *synonyms:* disapprove, condemn, criticize, belittle

tempestuous: adj. 1. stormy 2. (of a person) turbulent, violent, passionate
alt. forms: tempestuously - adv. tempestuousness - n.
synonyms: stormy, wild, uncontrollable, chaotic

Expressions for Discussion

1. *"Oh, this is the most tragical thing that ever happened to me!"* - Anne
   What is "the most tragical thing"? *finding out that she's not wanted because she's not a boy.*
2. *"If you'll only call me Anne spelled with an* e *I shall try to reconcile myself to not being called Cordelia."* - Anne
3. *"I'm in the depths of despair. Can you eat when you are in the depths of despair?"* - Anne
   Why is Anne in "the depths of despair"? *because she isn't wanted at Green Gables after thinking she had found a home*
4. *"We might be some good to her."* - Matthew Why were the Cuthberts adopting a child? *to help on the farm*
   How is Matthew's perspective about this changing? *Rather than thinking that a child could help him, he is thinking that he could help a child.*
5. *"Well now, she's a real interesting little thing."* - Matthew
   What do you think Matthew finds interesting about Anne? *her charm, imagination, complete guilelessness, dramatic flair, frankness, appreciation for nature, acceptance of him*

Comprehension Questions

Answer the following in complete sentences.

1. What is Marilla's surprise? What is Anne's reaction to Marilla's surprise? Marilla's surprise is the arrival of an orphan girl rather than a boy. Anne's reaction is to burst immediately into tears.

2. Who is Cordelia? Why does Anne insist that her name be spelled with an *e*? Cordelia is the name that Anne wants Marilla and Matthew to call her by because she thinks it is "a perfectly elegant name." She insists that her name be spelled with an *e* because she thinks it is much more distinguished and looks so much nicer.

3. Where does Marilla put Anne to bed? Marilla puts Anne to bed in the east gable room. (This would be a good time to introduce a picture of the house this novel was based on. A gable is a triangular section of wall between the edges of a sloping roof.)

4. How does Marilla know that Matthew is upset with the situation? Matthew is smoking, a clear sign of his troubled mind.

5. How does Matthew's perspective change concerning Anne? What causes his change of heart? *Matthew is dismayed when he sees that his orphan is a girl, but Anne immediately charms him. When Matthew and Marilla decided to adopt, it was in order to meet their needs, but when Matthew meets Anne, he begins to think about her needs. He sees that he and Marilla could make a difference in her life.

6. What is Marilla's reaction to Matthew's astonishing proposal? Marilla is astonished that Matthew would even consider keeping Anne. She thinks Anne has Matthew bewitched, and she is insistent that the child be returned to the orphanage because she will be of no good use to them.

Enrichment

1. Draw the White Way of Delight and the Lake of Shining Waters.

Yet Matthew wished to keep her, of all unaccountable things!

Reading Notes

Bonny	Anne's name for the apple-scented geranium
Snow Queen	Anne's name for the white cherry tree outside her bedroom window

Vocabulary

Write the meaning of each bold word or phrase.

1. "It's time you were dressed," she said **curtly**. n. noticeably or rudely brief
2. As it progressed Anne became more and more **abstracted** adj. preoccupied; lost in thought
3. with the most amazing silent **persistency** n. perseverance; stubbornness
4. if that's what you mean by **kindred** spirits n. similar in nature
5. in the tone of a **martyr** n. one who suffers or dies for a belief
6. Marilla **intercepted** the look v. interrupted; stopped

Expressions for Discussion

1. *"There was scope for imagination here."* - Anne
   Where is there scope for imagination? *at Green Gables*
   Why? *it's a beautiful, lovely place*
2. *"I'm not in the depths of despair this morning. I never can be in the morning."* - Anne
3. *"I think he's lovely … I felt that he was a kindred spirit as soon as ever I saw him."* - Anne
   What is Marilla's response to this statement? *"You're both queer enough, if that's what you mean by kindred spirits."*
4. *"She is kind of interesting, as Matthew says. I can feel already that I'm wondering what on earth she'll say next."* - Marilla
   What has Anne just been talking about that is "kind of interesting"? *her penchant for naming plants*

Comprehension Questions

Answer the following in complete sentences.

1. According to Anne, what is the "worst of imagining things"? The worst of imagining things is that there comes a time when you have to stop imagining and face reality, and that is painful.

2. What is it about Anne's silence at breakfast that makes Marilla nervous? As Anne eats in silence, she gradually becomes more and more withdrawn and abstracted, like her body is still at the breakfast table, but her spirit is in another place. This makes Marilla uncomfortable and nervous.

3. Why does Anne like to give names to everything, including geraniums? Anne feels it makes things seem more like people if she names them. Also, she is afraid they may get hurt feelings if they aren't named.

4. Why does Anne refuse to play outside when Marilla gives her permission? Anne doesn't want to fall in love with Green Gables because she knows she has to leave. It will be easier to leave if she isn't too attached to the place.

5. What is the spell Anne casts over Matthew and Marilla? Matthew and Marilla find Anne interesting and can't wait to hear what she has to say next. They are becoming attached to her so that they won't be able to let her go.

6. What makes Matthew wistful as Marilla and Anne drive away? Matthew does not want Anne to be returned to the orphanage. He is longing for a different resolution—one that lets him keep Anne in his life.

Enrichment

1. Matthew and Anne have very different personalities. Write a paragraph exploring the differences in their personalities and explain why you think they instantly like each other and could be "kindred spirits."

   Make two columns, labeled "Matthew" and "Anne." Then have students list character traits of each. Include similarities also, such as a love of nature. Lead students in seeing that Anne's volubility complements Matthew's shyness. This is a perfect example of opposites attracting.

Reading Notes

Mrs. Thomas	Anne's first foster parent after her parents died; harsh and unkind
Mrs. Hammond	Anne's second foster parent; made Anne work as a maid and nanny
Walter Shirley	Anne's father; a teacher at Bolingbroke High School
Bertha Shirley	Anne's mother

Vocabulary

Write the meaning of each bold word or phrase.

1. as you're evidently **bent** on talking ______ v. determined
2. called upon to **inculcate** a good and useful moral. ______ v. to persistently urge a particular idea or fact
3. "O-o-o-h," **faltered** Anne. ______ v. stammered, stumbled
4. to have twins three times in **succession** ______ n. one after another
5. a life of **drudgery** and poverty and neglect ______ n. tiresome, unpleasant work
6. their **pinions** flashing silvery in the sunlight. ______ n. wings

Expressions for Discussion

1. *"It's been my experience that you can nearly always enjoy things if you make up your mind firmly that you will."* - Anne

   What has Anne decided to enjoy? *the drive back to the orphanage*

2. *"Did you ever know of anybody whose hair was red when she was young, but got to be another color when she grew up?"* - Anne
3. *"My life is a perfect graveyard of buried hopes."* - Anne
4. *"If you'll only let me tell you what I imagine about myself you'll think it ever so much more interesting."* - Anne
5. *"I guess it doesn't matter what a person's name is as long as he behaves himself."* - Marilla
6. *"And when people mean to be good to you, you don't mind very much when they're not quite—always."* - Anne

   Do you think this is true? Are good intentions enough? *Mrs. Thomas appears to have done the best she could for Anne, given her circumstances, but Mrs. Hammond treated Anne as a slave. Anne is making a hurtful situation look as positive as possible because that is easier for her to live with.*

Comprehension Questions

Answer the following in complete sentences.

1. What is the hope that Anne has to place in her "graveyard of buried hopes"? Anne's lost hope is that her red hair will turn to a different color when she grows up.

2. How did Anne become an orphan? Anne's mother and father died of a fever when she was three months old. Her parents did not have any living relatives.

3. Why did Anne have to leave Mrs. Thomas' house? Why did Mrs. Hammond take her in? Mrs. Thomas was the woman who cleaned for Anne's parents. When they both died, she agreed to take Anne because no one else wanted her. When Mr. Thomas was killed, Mrs. Thomas went to live with her mother, who didn't want Anne. Mrs. Hammond agreed to take Anne so that she could help raise her eight children.

4. What kind of education has Anne received? Anne had very little formal schooling until she went to live at the orphanage. In her four months there, she did attend school.

5. How does Anne excuse Mrs. Thomas and Mrs. Hammond for not being good to her? Anne excuses Mrs. Thomas and Mrs. Hammond by saying that she is sure they meant to be good to her, but they had a great deal to worry about (Mrs. Thomas a drunken husband and Mrs. Hammond eight children), making it difficult for them to be good to her.

6. What effect does the story of Anne's past have on Marilla? Marilla is stirred by pity for Anne. She now understands that Anne has never been loved and sees that she and Matthew could indeed change this child's life. It is at this point that Marilla begins to seriously consider Matthew's wish to keep Anne.

7. At the end of this chapter, Anne says, "I don't want to get there. Somehow it will seem like the end of everything." What is ending for Anne? Anne's short time with Marilla and Matthew will be over when she and Marilla arrive at Mrs. Spencer's. It is the end of a dream that placed Anne in a home with loving people. To Anne, that is the end of everything.

Enrichment

1. Anne quotes from Shakespeare's *Romeo and Juliet* in this chapter. Read this dialogue between Romeo and Juliet in the play (Act II, Scene ii), and then memorize Juliet's speech (located in the Appendix) that includes the line Anne quotes: "a rose by any other name would smell as sweet."

Matthew's shy face was a glow of delight.

Reading Notes

Mrs. Peter Blewett woman who offers to take Anne in as a nanny; nasty and stingy

Robert Mrs. Spencer's brother who told her the Cuthberts wanted a girl orphan

Flora Jane Mrs. Spencer's daughter

Vocabulary

Write the meaning of each bold word or phrase.

1. welcome mingled on her **benevolent*** face. adj. eager to do good; charitable
2. A **blight** seemed to have descended on her. n. a harmful or destructive force
3. "She certainly did, Miss Cuthbert," **corroborated** Flora v. confirmed; supported
4. I call it positively **providential**. adj. marked by divine intervention
5. without an ounce of **superfluous*** flesh on her bones. adj. more than enough, excess
6. not daring to make any **stipulations** regarding the spelling n. requirements; demands

*Look up the following words in the dictionary, and write out the complete definition, the alternate forms, and 2-3 synonyms for each word.

benevolent: adj. 1. wishing to do good; actively friendly and helpful 2. charitable
alternate forms: benevolence - n. benevolently - adv.
synonyms: gracious, kind, friendly, cordial, congenial, considerate, altruistic

superfluous: adj. more than enough, redundant, needless
alternate forms: superfluously - adv. superfluousness - n.
synonyms: excessive, unneeded, unnecessary, redundant, extra

Expressions for Discussion

1. *"I didn't say that Matthew and I had absolutely decided that we wouldn't keep her."* - Marilla
   To whom is Marilla speaking? *Mrs. Blewett*
2. *"I'll try to do and be anything you want me, if you'll only keep me."* - Anne
3. *"I've been thinking over the idea until I've got kind of used to it. It seems a sort of duty."* - Marilla
   What is the idea Marilla has been thinking over? *raising Anne*
4. *"When I fail it'll be time enough to put your oar in."* - Marilla
   What does this expression mean? *The analogy here is of Matthew and Marilla in a boat. Marilla will steer and control the boat with her oar, but Matthew won't even have his oar in the water until given permission by Marilla. Anne is the boat being steered.*
5. *"I kind of think she's one of the sort you can do anything with if you only get her to love you."* - Matthew
   Why does Matthew think Anne will be easier to raise if they can get her to love them? *Anne is starved for love, and Matthew recognizes that she is the type of person who would respond to love with obedience and a desire to please.*

Comprehension Questions

Answer the following in complete sentences.

1. Who is responsible for the mistake made in bringing a girl back from the asylum? Why do you think the mistake was made? Marilla takes the blame for the mistake because she should have dealt with this important business herself rather than sending a messenger to do it for her. Mrs. Spencer's brother Robert gave Marilla's message to his daughter who gave it to Mrs. Spencer. Any time messages are passed through several people, the words are likely to get changed, many times taking on an entirely different meaning.

2. Why is Marilla hesitant to hand Anne over to Mrs. Blewett? Marilla has heard of Mrs. Blewett, who has the reputation of being stingy, bad-tempered, and a woman who works her servants hard. She knows that letting Anne be taken by Mrs. Blewett will place Anne back in the same situation she was in with Mrs. Hammond, a situation that caused Marilla to pity Anne. Finally, Marilla is afraid that if she lets Mrs. Blewett take Anne, she will be haunted by that decision.

3. Why is Mrs. Blewett anxious to take Anne with her? Mrs. Blewett wants Anne as a babysitter for her difficult baby.

4. What does Marilla think would "haunt her to her dying day"? Marilla thinks that ignoring the appeal in Anne's eyes, the look of "misery of a helpless creature who finds itself once more caught in the trap from which it had escaped" would haunt her.

5. Who is going to have all authority in the raising of Anne? What is the only thing Matthew asks of Marilla? *Marilla makes it clear to Matthew that she will have the authority in raising Anne without his interference. She only gives him permission to "put his oar in" after she has failed. Matthew asks Marilla to be as good and kind to Anne as she can without spoiling her.

Enrichment

1. Mrs. Spencer thinks it providential that Mrs. Blewett arrived just when Marilla had brought Anne back. This is providential, but not in the way Mrs. Spencer envisions. What is providence, and how has it worked in Anne's life?

   Providence is divine intervention. To Mrs. Spencer, Mrs. Blewett's arrival provided a divine solution to the problem of what to do with Anne. But providence is really at work here in Anne's life because Marilla may not have softened if she did not see for herself the situation that Anne was likely to end up in. So Mrs. Blewett's arrival lets Marilla see the need for her and Matthew to rescue Anne.

"You'd find it easier to be bad than good if you had red hair."

Vocabulary

Write the meaning of each bold word or phrase.

1. "… if you stay here," **admonished** Marilla. v. reprimanded, warned
2. responded Anne promptly and **glibly**. adv. in a smooth but insincere manner, superficially
3. by remembering that it was not **irreverence*** n. lack of reverence or due respect
4. responsible for this extraordinary **petition**. n. a request
5. She's next door to a perfect **heathen**. n. unbeliever; infidel
6. I'll send to the **manse** tomorrow n. residence of a minister

*Look up "reverence" and "irreverent" in the dictionary, and write out the complete definition of "irreverent," its alternate forms, and 2-3 synonyms.

adj. lacking reverence

alternate forms: irreverence - n. irreverential - adj. irreverently - adv.

synonyms: blasphemous, profane, disrespectful, insulting

Expressions for Discussion

1. *"I never say any prayers."* - Anne
2. *"People who haven't red hair don't know what trouble is. Mrs. Thomas told me that God made my hair red on purpose, and I've never cared about Him since."* - Anne
3. *"… And please let me be good-looking when I grow up."* - Anne
4. *"Well, well, we can't get through this world without our share of trouble. I've had a pretty easy life of it so far, but my time has come at last and I suppose I'll just have to make the best of it."* - Marilla
   What is the "share of trouble" that is facing Marilla now? *raising Anne, which Marilla knows will make her life more difficult*

Comprehension Questions

Answer the following in complete sentences.

1. Why does Anne decide she doesn't care for God? Mrs. Thomas told Anne that God had made her hair red on purpose so she has decided she doesn't care about Him.

2. What does Anne think would be the ideal way to pray? To Anne, the ideal way to pray would be to go into a big field or deep into the woods alone, look up into the lovely blue sky, and feel a prayer.

3. Why does Marilla decide a simple children's prayer will not be appropriate for Anne? Marilla realizes that a simple children's prayer would be inappropriate for Anne because she is not an innocent child. She comes from a life of difficulty and doesn't even know what love really is because she has never experienced it. She would get no benefit from a trite little prayer.

4. Based on the last paragraph of this chapter, do you think Marilla is looking forward to the challenge of raising Anne or dreading it? Explain your answer. Marilla appears to be enjoying the challenge of raising Anne. She is determined to take Anne in hand and teach her. This does not appear to be a burden to Marilla, but a difficult task that will bring great satisfaction.

Enrichment

1. Copy Anne's prayer in your best penmanship.

2. Draw Bonny and the Snow Queen.

"But it's a million times nicer to be Anne of Green Gables than Anne of nowhere in particular ..."

Reading Notes

Diana Barry a pretty girl Anne's age with black hair who lives next door to Green Gables
Mrs. Barry Diana's mother; strict

Vocabulary

Write the meaning of each bold word or phrase.

1. and said in an **imploring** voice adj. begging earnestly, entreating
2. unable to find an excuse for **deferring** her explanation v. postponing
3. and not stand stock-still and **discourse** about it. v. to converse; to talk
4. fell over the **rapt** little figure adj. delighted; deeply moved
5. Marilla had eyed that decoration **askance** adv. with a sideways glance of disgust or disapproval
6. studied **diligently*** for some moments longer. adv. showing care and effort

*Look up "diligent" in the dictionary, and write out the complete definition, the alternate forms, and 2-3 synonyms. adj. 1. careful and steady in application to one's work or duties
2. showing care and effort
alternate forms: diligently - adv.
synonyms: attentive, conscientious, hardworking, intent, steadfast, focused

Expressions for Discussion

1. *"It will be uphill work, I expect, for Mrs. Thomas often told me I was desperately wicked."* - Anne
   Who is Mrs. Thomas? *the scrubwoman who took Anne in after the death of her parents*
2. *"Oh, Miss—Marilla, how much you miss!"* - Anne
   Why does Marilla miss so much? *She doesn't use her imagination to imagine that things are different than they are.*
   What has Anne asked Marilla to imagine? *that she is Anne's aunt*
3. *"But I don't believe He could really have looked so sad or the children would have been afraid of Him."* - Anne
   Who looks sad? *Jesus*
4. *"What do you do when you meet with an irresistible temptation?"* - Anne
   What is Anne's "irresistible temptation"? *to pick flowers to put in the house*
5. *"But it's a million times nicer to be Anne of Green Gables than Anne of nowhere in particular, isn't it?"* - Anne
6. *"I don't approve of such goings-on. You seem to half believe your own imaginations."* - Marilla
   What is it that Marilla doesn't approve of? *Anne having imaginary friends*

Comprehension Questions

Answer the following in complete sentences.

1. What is Anne's chief shortcoming? Anne's chief shortcoming is her tendency to fall into daydreams in the middle of her tasks. This causes her to make mistakes or be reprimanded for not completing her tasks.

2. What does Marilla refuse to let Anne imagine? What is Anne's opinion of Marilla's refusal to imagine things differently than they really are? Marilla refuses to let Anne imagine that Marilla is her aunt. Anne thinks that Marilla misses so much in life because of her refusal to imagine that things are different than they really are. But Marilla thinks it is wrong to pretend that circumstances are different than they really are because God has placed us in those circumstances.

3. What does Marilla think is irreverent in Anne's imaginings of the picture of Christ? Marilla has a reverence and awe of God that makes it seem disrespectful for Anne to treat Jesus so familiarly. Anne is humanizing God too much for Marilla's comfort.

4. What is it that Anne simply could not endure in a bosom friend? Anne could not endure a bosom friend who had red hair.

5. What is the "moral" Marilla imparts to Anne about Diana? When Anne is concerned about Diana's appearance, Marilla tells her that Diana is "good and smart, which is better than being pretty." Marilla is attempting to show Anne that she is too caught up in physical appearances when she should be concentrating her energies on being a good person.

6. Who are Katie Maurice and Violetta? Katie Maurice is Anne's imaginary friend who lived in the bookcase at Mrs. Thomas' house. Violetta is Anne's imaginary friend who was an echo in a valley near Mrs. Hammond's house.

Enrichment

1. Imagine yourself in Marilla's picture of "Christ Blessing Little Children." Write your own story of how you would have felt in the presence of Christ.

Reading Notes

fortnight a period of 14 days; two weeks

Vocabulary

Write the meaning of each bold word or phrase.

1. all sorts of stories and **suppositions** n. assumptions; ideas
2. in all its delicious **vagaries** of brook and bridge n. strange ideas or acts
3. Her freckles were more numerous and **obtrusive** adj. unpleasantly noticeable
4. "Anne!" exclaimed Marilla in **consternation**. n. anxiety or dismay causing confusion
5. But Anne continued to face Mrs. Rachel **undauntedly** adv. without fear; courageously
6. she felt a most **reprehensible*** desire to laugh. adj. objectionable; unacceptable

*Look up "reprehensible" in the dictionary, and write out the complete definition, the alternate forms, and 2-3 synonyms. adj. deserving censure or rebuke; blameworthy
alternate forms: reprehensibility - n. reprehensibly - adv.
synonyms: objectionable, blameworthy

Expressions for Discussion

1. *"Well, they didn't pick you for your looks, that's sure and certain."* - Mrs. Lynde
   To whom is Mrs. Lynde speaking to? *Anne*
2. *"How dare you say such things about me? How would you like to have such things said about you?"* - Anne Who has said bad things about Anne? *Mrs. Lynde*
3. *"Oh, but there's such a difference between saying a thing yourself and hearing other people say it."* - Anne
4. *"You can shut me up in a dark, damp dungeon inhabited by snakes and toads and feed me only on bread and water and I shall not complain."* - Anne
   How can Anne get out of the "dungeon"? *by apologizing to Mrs. Lynde*

Comprehension Questions

Answer the following in complete sentences.

1. At what point does Marilla stop Anne from talking about her explorations of Avonlea? Why do you think this is? Marilla stops Anne's talk when she feels herself becoming too interested in it. Marilla is a person of reserve who takes the world seriously. Anne's imaginings and delight in the world make Marilla uncomfortable, so she fights against her interest in them.

2. Why is Mrs. Lynde intolerant of sickness except for grippe (influenza)? Mrs. Lynde is tolerant of grippe because she suffers from it. She is not a person of imagination, so she doesn't believe that any sickness she doesn't suffer from is worthy of attention. She only understands the suffering of a sickness she has endured.

3. Name the physical attributes Mrs. Lynde criticizes about Anne. What negative things does Anne say about Mrs. Lynde in response? Mrs. Lynde says that Anne wasn't chosen for her looks, is terribly skinny and homely, has lots of freckles, and hair that is as red as carrots. Anne retaliates by telling Mrs. Lynde that she is rude, impolite, unfeeling, fat, clumsy, and hasn't a spark of imagination.

4. What is the "serious defect" in Anne's disposition that Marilla discovers in this chapter? Marilla discovers that Anne has a terrible temper when pushed.

5. How does Mrs. Lynde, who has raised ten children, recommend that Marilla punish Anne? What punishment does Marilla actually impose upon Anne? Who shows better judgment here, the experienced mother or the inexperienced one? Mrs. Lynde thinks Marilla should spank Anne with a birch switch. Marilla doesn't believe she can whip a child, so the punishment she places on Anne is the requirement that Anne apologize to Mrs. Lynde. Marilla shows better judgment here because Anne's punishment suits her crime. Having to apologize to someone you have hurt is a good lesson in life.

6. Define "empathy." How does Marilla empathize with Anne in this chapter? Empathy is understanding someone's situation and feelings because you are able to identify with them. Marilla empathizes with Anne's anger and hurt when Mrs. Lynde says mean things about her because she remembers how she felt when she was a child and someone said something mean about her looks.

Enrichment

1. Research the meaning of a Parthian shaft. What was Marilla's Parthian shaft to Anne? In ancient times, the Parthians would pretend to retreat on horseback, and when their enemy pursued them, they would turn around in the saddle and shoot them with their bows. Marilla was retreating out of Anne's room, but her Parthian shaft as she walked out was "You said you would try to be a very good girl if we kept you at Green Gables, but I must say it hasn't seemed very much like it this evening."

2. Personification is a literary device in which inanimate objects are represented with human qualities or form. Find the personification in the fourth paragraph of this chapter. Gossamers glimmered like threads of silver among the trees and the fir boughs and tassels seemed **to utter friendly speech**.

"I thought since I had to do it I might as well do it thoroughly."

Vocabulary

Write the meaning of each bold word or phrase.

1. Anne proved still **refractory** the next morning adj. stubborn, rebellious
2. Anne still remained **obdurate**. adj. stubborn; obstinate
3. This was no meek **penitent*** n. a remorseful, repentant person
4. held out her hands **beseechingly**. adv. pleadingly; imploringly
5. revelling in the thoroughness of her **abasement**. n. humiliation; degradation
6. kindly, if somewhat **officious** heart. adj. excessively enthusiastic in offering help, meddlesome

*Look up "penitent" in the dictionary, and write out the complete definition, the alternate forms, and 2-3 synonyms. adj. & n. adj. regretting and wishing to atone for sins, repentant

n. a repentant sinner

alternate forms: penitence - n. penitently - adv.

synonyms: regretful, remorseful, sorrowful, sorry, contrite, apologetic

Expressions for Discussion

1. *"But don't be too hard on her, Marilla. Recollect she hasn't ever had anyone to teach her right."* - Matthew
2. *"When did you ever hear of me starving people into good behavior?"* - Marilla

   To what question is Marilla responding? *Matthew asked her if she was going to feed Anne while she is banished to her room.*
3. *"Of course, it's rather lonesome. But, then, I may as well get used to that."* - Anne

   Why is Anne lonesome? *She has been banished to her room.*
   To whom is she speaking? *Matthew*
4. *"You wouldn't like to inflict a lifelong sorrow on a poor little orphan girl, would you, even if she had a dreadful temper?"* - Anne

   To whom is Anne speaking? *Mrs. Lynde*
5. *"She might think I was putting my oar in and I promised not to do that."* - Matthew

   To whom is Matthew speaking? *Anne*
6. *"I apologized pretty well, didn't I? I thought since I had to do it I might as well do it thoroughly."* - Anne
   To whom is Anne speaking? *Marilla*

Comprehension Questions

Answer the following in complete sentences.

1. How does Matthew secretly "put his oar in"? How does he help Anne to give in to Marilla's demand? Matthew sneaks upstairs and asks Anne to apologize to Mrs. Lynde. This helps Anne to give in because she is now apologizing to oblige Matthew, who tells her he is lonely downstairs without her.

2. How long does Anne stay angry? How does she feel once her anger fades? Why does she feel she can't apologize to Mrs. Lynde? Anne stays angry throughout the night after she insulted Mrs. Lynde. She wakes up three times and is furious every time. But when she wakes up the next morning, she is no longer angry. She feels she can't apologize because it will be too humiliating.

3. How does Anne turn her apology from a humiliation into a triumph? Anne turns her apology into a performance. She acts the part of a repentant, and it is a triumph because Mrs. Lynde falls for every word.

4. What does Marilla perceive about Anne's apology that Mrs. Lynde does not perceive? Marilla is more perceptive than Mrs. Lynde and does not fall for Anne's apology. She recognizes it for what it is—an excellent performance. Marilla sees that Anne is thoroughly enjoying herself in her role.

5. How does Mrs. Lynde respond to Anne's apology? What is Marilla's response? Mrs. Lynde heartily forgives Anne and even tells Marilla that maybe she hasn't made a mistake in adopting Anne after all. She says that because Anne has a quick temper, she will probably never be deceitful. Marilla finds herself amused with Anne's apology and her ability to outtalk Mrs. Lynde, but she doesn't let Anne know that she has amused her. Instead, she gives Anne a lecture on controlling her temper.

6. Name one or two morals that Marilla imparts to Anne in this chapter.
   "Handsome is as handsome does."
   "If you'll be a good girl, you'll always be happy."

Enrichment

1. On a separate sheet of paper, copy Anne's apology in your best penmanship.
2. Draw a picture of Green Gables at night as it would have looked to you if you had been walking home from Mrs. Lynde's with Anne and Marilla.

Anne felt that life was really not worth living without puffed sleeves.

Reading Notes

Mr. Bell	the church superintendent; leads a prayer every Sunday, which Anne finds boring and unimpassioned
Miss Rogerson	Anne's Sunday school teacher; asks many questions

Vocabulary

Write the meaning of each bold word or phrase.

1. without any frills or **furbelows** about them n. ruffles or frills on a skirt or petticoat
2. disappearing downstairs in high **dudgeon**. n. a feeling of great resentment; rage
3. she whispered **disconsolately**. adv. in an unhappy or disappointed manner
4. holding her **ruddy** head with its decoration adj. rosy; healthy
5. "Anne Shirley!" said Marilla **rebukingly**. adv. reproachfully; disapprovingly
6. she was **hampered** by the undeniable fact v. prevented or hindered

Expressions for Discussion

1. *"I'll imagine that I like them."* - Anne
   What is Anne imagining that she will like? *her new dresses without puffed sleeves*
2. *"It would give me such a thrill, Marilla, just to wear a dress with puffed sleeves."* - Anne
3. *"I didn't suppose God would have time to bother about a little orphan girl's dress."* - Anne
4. *"You shouldn't have been thinking about your sleeves in Sunday school."* - Marilla

Comprehension Questions

Answer the following in complete sentences.

1. Describe the dresses Marilla makes for Anne. What does Anne attempt to imagine about the dresses that she wants very badly? Anne's new dresses are all alike—plain skirts fitted tightly to plain waists with plain, tight sleeves. Anne attempts to imagine that she likes them.

2. What was Anne's prayer that God did not answer? Why does Anne think God did not answer her prayer? Anne prayed for a white dress with puffed sleeves. She thinks God did not answer her prayer because he doesn't have time to bother with a little orphan girl's dress.

3. How does Anne change her appearance on the way to Sunday school? Anne makes a wreath of pink and yellow wildflowers that she uses to garland her hat.

4. What does Anne think about the sermon? What does she think the trouble with the minister is? Anne feels the sermon is too long and not a bit interesting. She thinks this is because the minister doesn't have enough imagination.

5. Why does Marilla not reprove Anne's comments about the minister and Mr. Bell's prayer? Marilla thinks that some of the criticisms that Anne makes about the minister's sermons and Mr. Bell's prayers are true and what she herself has thought for years but never expressed.

Enrichment

1. Paraphrases were rhymed portions of scripture sung without musical accompaniment in the Scottish churches. Copy the paraphrase, *The Race That Long In Darkness Pined* (located in the Appendix), that Anne had to recite in Sunday School. Then copy the original scripture this paraphrase is taken from (Isaiah 9:2-8). What is the theme of the paraphrase? Recite this paraphrase as Anne would have done.

   The theme of this paraphrase is the coming of Jesus as Savior of the world.

"Will you swear to be my friend for ever and ever?"

Reading Notes

Dryad's Bubble Anne and Diana's name for the spring by the log bridge

Carmody the nearby town Matthew visits and brings home candy from

Vocabulary

Write the meaning of each bold word or phrase.

1. from the safe concrete into **dubious** paths of the abstract. adj. uncertain, unreliable
2. **vexed** at herself for having made the child cry. adj. angered; irritated
3. slipped **unheeded** to the floor. adj. disregarded, unnoticed
4. with a very **resolute*** mouth. adj. determined; decided
5. **tremulous** and excited as she was adj. timid; fearful
6. **beguiled** into loitering v. distracted; charmed; entranced

*Look up "resolute" in the dictionary, and write out the complete definition, the alternate forms, and 2-3 synonyms. adj. determined; decided; firm in purpose; not vacillating

alternate forms: resolutely - adv. resoluteness - n.

synonyms: resolved, purposeful, stubborn, adamant, persistent

Expressions for Discussion

1. *"I don't think I could endure it; most likely I would go into consumption; I'm so thin as it is, you see. But that would be better than being a trial to you."* - Anne
   What could Anne not endure? *returning to the orphanage to live*
2. *"It would be the most tragical disappointment of my life."* - Anne
   What would be Anne's "most tragical disappointment"? *if Diana doesn't like her*
3. *"I am well in body although considerably rumpled up in spirit, thank you, ma'am."* - Anne
   To whom is Anne speaking? *Mrs. Barry*
4. *"You're a queer girl, Anne. I heard before that you were queer. But I believe I'm going to like you real well."* - Diana
5. *"Dear me, it's only three weeks since she came, and it seems as if she's been here always. I can't imagine the place without her."* - Marilla

Comprehension Questions

Answer the following in complete sentences.

1. Why does Anne not think it is ridiculous to wear flowers in her hat to church? Why is it inappropriate for Anne to wear flowers in her hat? Many of the other girls had flowers on their dresses and Anne doesn't see the difference in having flowers on one's hat and having them on one's dress. The other girls had tasteful flowers that complemented their apparel, while Anne had placed a bunch of wildflowers around her hat, which stood out in disarray and appeared showy. This would be considered inappropriate church attire.
2. What does Anne think is better than being a "trial" to Marilla? Anne thinks it would be better to be returned to the orphanage rather than continuing to be a trial to Marilla.
3. What would be "the most tragical disappointment" of Anne's life? The most tragical disappointment of Anne's life would be if Diana Barry doesn't like her and her dream of a bosom friend is not realized.
4. What are the two kinds of swearing? What kind of oath do Anne and Diana swear? In Anne's opinion, the bad kind of swearing is when one uses profanity or curses. The good kind of swearing is when one makes a vow or promise. Anne and Diana swear to be faithful bosom friends forever
5. How is Anne's dilemma of not having any gift to give Diana solved? Matthew brings Anne some chocolate candy from Carmody, so Anne gives half of it to Diana as a gift.
6. What good quality does Marilla discover about Anne's character in this chapter? Marilla discovers that Anne is not stingy when Anne saves half of her candy for Diana.

Enrichment

1. Make a list of the flowers and plants growing in the Barrys' garden.
   tiger lilies, rosy bleeding-hearts, crimson peonies, white narcissi, Scotch roses, columbines, Bouncing Bets, southernwood, ribbon grass, mint, purple Adam-and-Eve, daffodils, feathery sprays, scarlet lightning, white musk-flowers
2. Draw a picture of the Dryad's Bubble.

"... think of it, Marilla—ice-cream!"

Reading Notes

Idlewild	Anne and Diana's name for their playhouse
Willowmere	Anne and Diana's name for the little round pool in Mr. Barry's field

Vocabulary

Write the meaning of each bold word or phrase.

1. behind her in a **torrent** of brightness. n. outpouring; flow
2. rapturously kissed her **sallow** cheek. adj. a sickly yellow
3. the reason why she said **brusquely** adv. abruptly; bluntly
4. "I do not like patchwork," said Anne **dolefully** adv. with mourning or sadness
5. she went through great **tribulations**. n. trials; sufferings
6. who in turn had **bequeathed** it to Marilla. v. left to a person by will; handed down

Expressions for Discussion

1. *"I never saw such an infatuated man. The more she talks and the odder the things she says, the more he's delighted evidently."* - Marilla
   Who is the "infatuated man"? *Matthew*

2. *"Matthew is such a sympathetic listener."* - Anne
   About what has Anne been talking to Matthew? *the church picnic*

3. *"I have to furnish most of the imagination, but I'm well able to do that."* - Anne
   Who does not have a vivid imagination like Anne? *Diana*

4. *"I stayed awake nearly a whole night before I invented it. Then, just as I was dropping off to sleep, it came like an inspiration."* - Anne
   What kept Anne up all night? *trying to think of a good name for the ring of birch trees; she named it Idlewild*

5. *"The heroine had five lovers. I'd be satisfied with one, wouldn't you?"* - Anne
   To whom is Anne talking? *Marilla*

6. *"I'd love to be able to faint, wouldn't you, Marilla? It's so romantic."* - Anne

Comprehension Questions

Answer the following in complete sentences.

1. Why is Marilla exasperated with Matthew? Marilla thinks Matthew is infatuated with Anne and lets her get away with anything. Marilla is angry because Anne should be inside doing her chores, but Matthew is letting her stay outside and talk to him as long as she will talk.

2. What is the most exciting thing to Anne about the church picnic? The most exciting thing about the picnic is that they are going to serve ice cream.

3. What would be Anne's "lifelong sorrow" in this chapter? If Anne misses the picnic, it will be a "lifelong sorrow," even though she does think she will live through the disappointment.

4. Why doesn't Anne like sewing patchwork? Why does she have to sew an extra square on Saturday? Anne dislikes patchwork because there is no scope for the imagination in it. It is just one seam after another with no creativity involved. Anne has to sew an extra square on Saturday as a way of steadying her nerves since it is raining and she is very nervous about the rain continuing through the picnic on Wednesday.

5. What color do you think amethysts are, based on Anne's question, "Do you think amethysts can be the souls of good violets?" Why was Anne disappointed the first time she saw a diamond? Amethysts are purple. Anne was disappointed the first time she saw a diamond because it was colorless and she had imagined that diamonds were purple.

Enrichment

1. Marilla tells Anne that she sets her "heart too much on things" and that she's afraid there will be "a great many disappointments in store" for her. Anne responds that "it would be worse to expect nothing than to be disappointed." Write a paragraph explaining both Marilla's and Anne's viewpoints. Include your opinion of the best way to live and explain your reasoning.

   Marilla thinks that if you don't have expectations, then you will not be disappointed when great things don't happen to you. But for Anne, much of the thrill is in the anticipation of good things.

2. Draw Idlewild and Willowmere.

"He felt no desire to put his oar in this time."

Vocabulary

Write the meaning of each bold word or phrase.

1. Matthew was **confounded** v. confused
2. without the least apparent **compunction** or repentance. n. guilty conscience
3. feebly **reiterated** Matthew. v. repeated
4. what that **rigmarole** you told me this morning meant. n. a rambling or meaningless story
5. in a state of **beatification** impossible to describe. n. making or being blessed
6. I assure you it was **sublime***. adj. supreme; splendid

*Look up "sublime" in the dictionary, and write out the complete definition, the alternate forms, and 2-3 synonyms. adj. & v. adj. 1. of the most exalted, grand, or noble kind; awe inspiring 2. arrogantly unruffled; extreme v. to purify or elevate by or as if by sublimation; to make sublime *alternate forms:* sublimely - adv. sublimity - n. *synonyms:* lofty, high, supreme, exalted, elevated

Expressions for Discussion

1. *"That's one good thing about me. I never do the same naughty thing twice."* - Anne
   What was Anne's naughty action that she will never repeat? *trying on Marilla's brooch without permission*

2. *"That's the plain, ugly truth, Matthew Cuthbert, and we might as well look it in the face."* - Marilla
   What is "the plain, ugly truth"? *Marilla believes Anne has lied to her.*

3. *"You'll feel remorse of conscience some day, I expect, for breaking it, Marilla, but I forgive you."* - Anne
   What has Marilla broken? *Anne's heart* How did Marilla break it? *by not allowing Anne to attend the picnic*

4. *"Boiled pork and greens are so unromantic when one is in affliction."* - Anne

5. *"I thought out a confession last night after I went to bed and made it as interesting as I could."* - Anne
   What is Anne confessing to? *losing Marilla's brooch*

6. *"And there's one thing certain, no house will ever be dull that she's in."* - Marilla

Comprehension Questions

Answer the following in complete sentences.

1. What troubles Marilla more than the missing brooch? More troublesome to Marilla than losing her brooch is the fact that Anne may have taken it and lied to her about it.

2. How does Marilla attempt to solve the problem of the missing brooch? What conclusion does she finally come to? Marilla searches the house and comes to the conclusion that Anne has to have taken her brooch. She makes Anne stay in her room until she confesses to the crime.

3. In what way does Matthew refuse to "put his oar in" this time? Marilla tells Matthew that Anne will have to be severely punished once she has confessed to taking the brooch. Matthew reminds Marilla that he is not to interfere in the raising of Anne, so he will not have to be the one inflicting punishment on her.

4. Reread Anne's confession. What is suspicious about it that should have made Marilla think twice about the truth of it? Anne delivers her confession as if repeating a memorized lesson. Her recitation is calm and unrepentant. Marilla should recognize that this is completely out of character for Anne.

5. After the brooch is found, Marilla admits that she was wrong. What was her first mistake? Marilla admits that her first mistake was in doubting Anne's honesty when Anne had never lied to her before. She should have trusted what she knew of Anne's character before accusing Anne unfairly.

Enrichment

1. Read Luke 9:57-62. Find the quote in this chapter that comes from this passage. What does this verse mean, and how does it apply to Marilla and Anne?

   "Oh dear, I'm afraid Rachel was right from the first. But I've put my hand to the plough and I won't look back." - Marilla

   Putting your hand to the plow and not looking back means that you will persevere in whatever goal or task you have set for yourself. Jesus is telling the man that he needs to keep his eyes fixed on Him and not on things of the earth. Marilla borrows from this verse to say that even though it looks like Rachel Lynde was correct in her first criticism of Matthew and Marilla's adoption of a child, Marilla has committed to raising Anne and she will persevere. She will not give up now but will complete her task to the best of her abilities.

Reading Notes

Mr. Phillips	the Avonlea schoolmaster; inattentive teacher
Gilbert Blythe	Anne's classmate who mocks her red hair, thus becoming her rival
Prissy Andrews	Anne's sixteen-year-old classmate; courted by Mr. Phillips
Violet Vale	Anne's name for the "green dimple" in the shadow of Mr. Bell's woods

Vocabulary

Write the meaning of each bold word or phrase.

1. Beyond Willowmere came Violet **Vale** ______ n. valley
2. off the old pincushion in the **garret** ______ n. attic
3. tripping **blithely*** down the Birch Path ______ adv. light-heartedly; carelessly
4. winked with inexpressible **drollery**. ______ n. comedy; clowning
5. still with the sarcastic **inflection** ______ n. a change in the pitch of the voice
6. **ostentatiously*** took out everything ______ adv. in a showy, boastful manner

*Look up the following words in the dictionary, and write out the complete definitions, the alternate forms, and 2-3 synonyms for each word.

blithe: adj. 1. happy, joyful 2. careless, casual
alt. forms: blithely - adv. blitheness - n. blithesome - adj.
synonyms: blissful, cheerful, joyous, lighthearted, carefree, indifferent

ostentation: n. 1. a pretentious and vulgar display, esp. of wealth and luxury 2. the attempt or intention to attract notice; showing off *alt. forms:* ostentatious - adj. ostentatiously - adv.
synonyms: showy, boastful, pretentious, vain

Expressions for Discussion

1. *"But there's not one of them has such an imagination as I have, and I soon found that out."* - Anne
   Who is the group Anne is speaking about? *her schoolmates*

2. *"Marilla, that is the first compliment I have ever had in my life and you can't imagine what a strange feeling it gave me."* - Anne
   What is the compliment Anne has received? *Prissy Andrews said she had a pretty nose.*

3. *"I'd rather be pretty than clever."* - Anne

4. *"And Mr. Phillips spelled my name without an* e *too. The iron has entered into my soul, Diana."* - Anne

5. *"I'd let myself be torn limb from limb if it would do you any good. But I can't do this, so please don't ask it. You harrow up my very soul."* - Anne

Who is "harrowing up" Anne's soul? *Diana* How? *by begging Anne not to quit school*

6. *"Well, Anne Shirley, if you must borrow trouble, for pity's sake borrow it handier home. I should think you had an imagination, sure enough."* - Marilla

What is the trouble Anne has borrowed? *worry about Diana getting married one day and leaving her*

Comprehension Questions

Answer the following in complete sentences.

1. What is Marilla's secret misgiving as Anne starts off to school? Marilla is afraid that Anne is so strange that she won't be able to get along with the other children. She is also afraid that Anne won't be able to keep her mouth closed during the school hours.

2. Who does Mr. Phillips favor? Who is his scapegoat? Mr. Phillips favors Prissy Andrews because he is sweet on her. Anne is his scapegoat. He punishes her even though Gilbert tries to take the blame for inciting Anne to misbehavior.

3. What are "Take Notices"? Even though Anne doesn't want her name written up, what does she find "a little humiliating"? A "Take Notice" is a public notice placed on a wall, coupling a boy's name with a girl's, announcing a romantic attachment between them. Anne thinks it is humiliating that there is no danger of her name being placed on a Take Notice with a boy's even though she doesn't want to be coupled with a boy.

4. Who comes to school three weeks into the term? What is Anne's impression of him? Gilbert Blythe comes to school three weeks into the term. Anne thinks that he is handsome, but very bold because he winks at her.

5. What does Gilbert do to Anne, and how does she retaliate? What is her punishment? Gilbert calls Anne "Carrots" to get her attention. She calls him a "mean, hateful boy" and slams him in the head with her slate. Her punishment is to stand on the platform in front of the blackboard all afternoon with a notice over her head that names her crime and misspells her name.

6. What causes Marilla to laugh like she has never laughed before? Marilla is highly amused that Anne has worked herself into a crying state over Diana one day marrying and leaving Anne all alone.

Enrichment

1. Draw the Avonlea classroom. Then draw your classroom. What are the differences?

Reading Notes

cordial strong highly flavored sweet liquor usually drunk after a meal

Vocabulary

Write the meaning of each bold word or phrase.

1. Anne **revelled** in the world of color about her. v. delighted
2. whose **aesthetic*** sense was not noticeably developed. adj. having to do with beauty
3. to bury a broken heart in **cloistered** seclusion. adj. sheltered; secluded
4. Anne sat up, tragedy **personified**. adj. embodied in human form
5. a white-lipped, eager-eyed **supplicant** on the doorstep. n. humble beggar
6. drunk out of sheer malice **prepense** adj. intentional, premeditated; planned

*Look up "aesthetic" in the dictionary, and write out the complete definition, the alternate forms, and 2-3 synonyms. adj. & n. adj. 1. concerned with beauty or the appreciation of beauty 2. having such appreciation; sensitive to beauty 3. in accordance with the principles of good taste n. 1. (in pl.) philosophy of the beautiful 2. a set of principles of good taste *alt. forms:* aesthetically - adv. aestheticism - n. *synonyms:* artistic, refined, discriminating, cultivated

Expressions for Discussion

1. *"I'm so glad I live in a world where there are Octobers. It would be terrible if we just skipped from September to November, wouldn't it?"* - Anne
2. *"Bedrooms were made to sleep in."* - Marilla
3. *"Matthew would think it all right, Anne, if you took a notion to get up and have dinner in the middle of the night."* - Marilla
4. *"There's so little scope for imagination in cookery. You just have to go by rules."* - Anne

   To whom is Anne speaking? *Diana*
5. *"The stars in their courses fight against me, Marilla."* - Anne

   How are the stars fighting against Anne? *She has made Diana drunk, so they are parted forever.*
6. *"... You will cover my life with a dark cloud of woe."* - Anne

   Who is covering Anne's life with "a dark cloud of woe"? *Mrs. Barry*
   How? *by separating Anne and Diana forever*
7. *"I do not believe that God Himself can do very much with such an obstinate person as Mrs. Barry."* - Marilla

Comprehension Questions

Answer the following in complete sentences.

1. Why did Anne forget to put the tea on to brew the last time she was responsible for Matthew's tea? How did she entertain him while he waited? Anne was trying to think of a name for Violet Vale, which made her forget to brew Matthew's tea. But she entertained Matthew with a story of fairies while they waited for it to brew.

2. What was Anne daydreaming about when she forgot to put the flour in the cake? Anne was imagining that Diana was desperately ill with smallpox and Anne was the only one brave enough to go to her bedside and nurse her back to health. But then Anne took smallpox and died, and Diana planted a rosebush by her grave and watered it with her tears. This daydream caused Anne to forget to put the flour in the cake.

3. Why did Anne neglect to cover the pudding sauce? Anne was imagining that she was a nun who had taken the veil in order to bury her broken heart, so she forgot to put the cover on the pudding sauce.

4. Whose fault is it that Anne gets Diana drunk? Who does Marilla blame it on? Marilla told Anne the cordial was in the wrong place, so it was really Marilla's fault that Anne gave Diana currant wine instead of raspberry cordial. But Marilla blames the mistake on Diana who was greedy enough to drink three large glasses.

5. Name some of Mrs. Barry's character traits. Mrs. Barry is a woman of strong prejudices and dislikes. She has a cold, sullen kind of anger that is hard to overcome. She is a protective mother, but an unforgiving one. She is harsh to Anne and has a suspicious nature that keeps her from being able to see the sincerity in Anne's heartfelt apology.

Enrichment

1. Narrate the story of the plum pudding in your own words.

2. Look up Proverbs 25:22 and Romans 12:20. Anne says that being offered strawberry preserves by Marilla was "like heaping coals of fire on my head." What does this expression mean? Relate it to Anne's experience.

   If you are forgiving and consistently nice in the face of being mistreated by others, you prove yourself to be a person of moral strength and character. As Paul says in Romans 12:21, you are overcoming evil with good. Marilla is repaying Anne's misbehavior with the reward of strawberry preserves. Anne feels the injustice of being rewarded for her mistake, as if Marilla is heaping coals of fire on her head.

"I thought you liked *me, of course, but I never hoped you* loved *me."*

Vocabulary

Write the meaning of each bold word or phrase.

1. said Diana **staunchly*** adv. faithfully, loyally
2. her dramatic ability in the **perusal** aloud of books n. careful reading
3. the following **effusion** n. an outpouring, unrestrained flow
4. annexed it as one of his **perquisites**. n. extra benefits, customary privileges
5. gorgeously **bedizened** with striped red and yellow paper v. adorned gaudily
6. an unpraiseworthy **tenacity*** for holding grudges. n. unwillingness to let go, stubbornness

*Look up the following words in the dictionary and write out the complete definition, the alternate forms, and 2-3 synonyms for each word:

staunch: adj. 1. trustworthy, loyal 2. strong, watertight, airtight
alternate forms: staunchly - adv. staunchness - n.
synonyms: steadfast, loyal, dependable, reliable, constant, faithful

tenacious: adj. 1. keeping a firm hold of property, principles, life; not readily relinquishing 2. (of memory) retentive 3. holding fast 4. strongly cohesive 5. persistent, resolute
alt. forms: tenaciously - adv. tenaciousness - n. tenacity - n. *syn.:* persistent, determined, diligent

Expressions for Discussion

1. *"Ten minutes isn't very long to say an eternal farewell in."* - Anne
   To whom is Anne saying an "eternal farewell"? *Diana*
2. *"Please see that it is buried with me, for I don't believe I'll live very long."* - Anne
   What is to go into Anne's grave with her? *a lock of Diana's hair*
3. *"If you're going back to school I hope we'll hear no more of breaking slates over people's heads and such carryings-on."* - Marilla
4. *"There is no scope for imagination in it at all. Mr. Phillips says I'm the worst dunce he ever saw at it."* - Anne
   What is there "no scope for imagination in" this time? *geometry*
5. *"... One can't stay sad very long in such an interesting world, can one?"* - Anne

Comprehension Questions

Answer the following in complete sentences.

1. What does Anne decide to do as a result of her forced separation from Diana? What is Marilla's reaction to Anne's decision? Anne has decided to return to school because that is all that is left in life for her. At least in school she can see Diana. Marilla is delighted at this turn of events because she never wanted Anne to drop out of school in the first place.

2. According to Anne, what qualities is Mr. Phillips looking for in a "model pupil"? Do you think it is realistic for Anne to think she can live up to these expectations and become a model pupil herself? Mr. Phillips considers model students to be those who have no imagination or life in them and are dull and never seem to have a good time. Anne thinks that she is so depressed over her loss of Diana that she can be one of those model students. This is not realistic because Anne will never be a person without vitality or energy; it is not in her character.

3. Who becomes Anne's academic rival in the classroom? Which subject is her biggest challenge? What is it about this subject that makes it so awful to Anne? Gilbert Blythe becomes Anne's academic rival. Geometry is the subject that she struggles with. She says it is awful because there is no scope for imagination in it. Unlike the poetry that Anne loves to dissect and interpret in various ways, geometry is what it is and cannot be changed.

4. The title of this chapter is "A New Interest in Life." What is Anne's new interest? Does she use the tragedy of her separation from Diana as a stepping stone or a stumbling block? Anne's new interest in life is academics. She applies herself to become a stellar student. She uses her separation from Diana as a stepping stone as she concentrates her energies on her education.

Enrichment

1. The author says, "In geometry Anne met her Waterloo." Explain this statement. What happened at Waterloo, and how does this relate to Anne's experience with geometry?
   Napoleon, who looked powerful enough to conquer the world at one time, met his defeat and capture at Waterloo, marking the end of his rule as emperor of the French. Geometry threatens to be Anne's Waterloo, marking the end of a promising academic career.

"This is the last lingering hope and I fear 'tis a vain one."

Reading Notes

Premier	the chief administrative officer of Avonlea
Minnie May	Diana's little sister; falls ill with croup
croup	respiratory disease affecting the larynx that causes inflammation, which obstructs breathing
Liberal	political party associated with social and political liberalism
Conservative	political party associated with social and political conservatism

Vocabulary

Write the meaning of each bold word or phrase.

1. she's going to have ever so many **beaux** on the string n. (pl. of beau) admirers, boyfriends
2. Has your mother **relented** at last? v. yielded to compassion, shown mercy
3. friend who had been so long **estranged***. v. alienated; separated
4. Anne's **consequent** excitement would lift her adj. logically consistent
5. her face **irradiated** with the flame of her spirit. v. shone upon, lit up
6. dark **glens** of spruce. n. narrow, secluded valleys

*Look up "estrange" in the dictionary, and write out the complete definition, the alternate forms, and 2-3 synonyms. v. to turn away in feeling or affection, alienate

alternate forms: estrangement - n.

synonyms: alienated, divided, separated, driven apart, disassociated

Expressions for Discussion

1. *"It is casting a cloud over my whole life."* - Anne
   What is "casting a cloud" over Anne's whole life? *geometry*
2. *"It's all very well to say resist temptation, but it's ever so much easier to resist it if you can't get the key."*
   - Anne To whom is Anne talking? *Matthew*
   What kind of temptation is Anne trying to overcome? *the temptation to read a novel rather than doing her homework*
3. *"Matthew and I are such kindred spirits I can read his thoughts without words at all."* - Anne
   To whom is Anne speaking? *Diana*
4. *"She seems to have a skill and presence of mind perfectly wonderful in a child of her age."*
   - the doctor About whom is he speaking? *Anne*
5. *"I can tell by the look of you that you're just full up with speeches, but they'll keep."* - Marilla
6. *"I cannot tie myself down to anything so unromantic as dish-washing at this thrilling moment."* - Anne
   What is the "thrilling moment"? *Mrs. Barry has forgiven Anne and will allow her and Diana to be friends again.*
7. *"I'm perfectly happy—yes, in spite of my red hair. Just at present I have a soul above red hair."* - Anne

Comprehension Questions

Answer the following in complete sentences.

1. Why does Rachel Lynde choose to go to the political rally even though it is not her political party? What is Mrs. Lynde's political party? To which party do Matthew and Marilla belong? Rachel Lynde is so interested in politics that she feels a political rally can't take place without her attendance, even if it is not a rally for her party. Rachel Lynde is a member of the Liberal party and Matthew and Marilla are Conservatives.
2. Anne is tempted to read her book instead of doing her geometry. What is her primary motivation for resisting? Anne's primary motivation for studying geometry rather than reading for pleasure is so that Gilbert won't triumph over her in class the next day.
3. Anne tells the doctor that "there are some things that cannot be expressed in words." What is it that she can't express in words? Anne can't express her relief that Minnie May has lived through the night. The feelings are too deep to be represented by mere words.
4. Why is croup so frightening? Why does Anne know how to treat croup? It can result in death if the airways get completely obstructed and the child can't breathe. Anne knows how to treat croup because of her past experience with the Hammond twins.
5. After reading the entire chapter, explain the meaning of the first sentence: "All things great are wound up with all things little." The small circumstance of so many adults being away for a political rally leaves Anne responsible for Minnie May's recovery. But this small circumstance ultimately leads to the great reunion of Anne and Diana due to Mrs. Barry's thankfulness to Anne.

Enrichment

1. Anne's miserable experience of taking care of three sets of twins turns out to be fortuitous for Minnie May. What does "fortuitous" mean? Do most of our valuable learning experiences come when we are having fun or doing something difficult and even unpleasant?

   Fortuitous is a happening by chance or accident. It was a happy chance that Anne knew how to treat croup.

2. In this chapter, Anne heaps coals of fire on Mrs. Barry's head. Add an explanation of this reference to your paragraph from Chapter 16 that deals with this scripture reference.

   *Anne heaps coals of fire on Mrs. Barry's head by totally forgiving her even though Mrs. Barry was unwilling to do the same for Anne when she got Diana drunk.

"I'd rather walk up to a cannon's mouth."

Reading Notes

Josephine Barry	Diana's rich aunt who lives in a mansion in Charlotteville; charmed by Anne
pung sleigh	a low one-horse box sleigh

Vocabulary

Write the meaning of each bold word or phrase.

1. said **tartly**: "Very well, she can go." adv. sharply; bitterly
2. when they got home, **sated** v. satisfied; gratified
3. with **dissipation**, but with the exceeding sweet pleasure n. frivolous living
4. It's because you're too **heedless** adj. thoughtless; unmindful
5. She shook her head **sagely**. adv. wisely
6. after a long and **arduous*** journey adj. hard to achieve; difficult

*Look up "arduous" in the dictionary, and write out the complete definition, the alternate forms, and 2-3 synonyms. adj. 1. hard to achieve or overcome; difficult; laborious 2. energetic, strenuous

alternate forms: arduously - adv. arduousness - n.

synonyms: difficult, tough, strenuous, burdensome, backbreaking

Expressions for Discussion

1. *"It ain't interfering to have your own opinion. And my opinion is that you ought to let Anne go."* - Matthew Where does Matthew think Anne should go? *to the Debating Club concert for Diana's birthday*
2. *"I'm Anne of Green Gables, and I've come to confess, if you please."* - Anne To whom is she confessing? *Miss Josephine Barry*
3. *"I've been so used in my early days to having people cross at me that I can endure it much better than Diana can."* - Anne
4. *"But just imagine what you would feel like if you were a little orphan girl who had never had such an honor."* - Anne What is the honor the "little orphan girl" had? *to sleep in a spare room*
5. *"... You seem like an interesting lady, and you might even be a kindred spirit although you don't look very much like it."* - Anne Who might be a "kindred spirit"? *Miss Barry*
6. *"Miss Marilla Cuthbert is a very kind lady who has taken me to bring up properly. She is doing her best, but it is very discouraging work."* - Anne
7. *"She amuses me, and at my time of life an amusing person is a rarity."* - Miss Barry What do you think is amusing about Anne to Miss Barry? *her dramatic flair, frank honesty, conversational style*

Comprehension Questions

Answer the following in complete sentences.

1. Name the reasons Anne gives for needing to go to the Debating Club concert. Anne says the concert is a respectable affair, the recitations are moral pieces, the choir is going to sing songs that are almost as good as hymns, and the minister is speaking, which is almost like having a sermon. She also points out the fact that Diana only has one birthday a year. Anne's final attempt is to tell Marilla that she would get the honor of sleeping in the Barrys' spare room.

2. Name the reasons Marilla is opposed to Anne's attending the concert. Why does Marilla change her mind and let Anne go? Marilla thinks the concert is nonsense and Anne would be better off in her own bed. She thinks it is an inappropriate affair for children to attend and that children shouldn't be staying out all hours of the night. Matthew convinces Marilla to let Anne go to the concert. He doesn't fight with Marilla; he just states his simple case repeatedly: "I think you ought to let Anne go." Finally, he wears Marilla down and she agrees to let Anne go.

3. What do Anne and Diana discover in the Barrys' spare bedroom, and how is this discovery made? Anne and Diana discover Diana's Aunt Josephine in the spare bedroom bed when they leap onto her at the end of their race to see who can get to the bed first.

4. What is Anne's confession? Anne confesses to Aunt Josephine that it is her fault that she and Diana leaped onto the bed. Anne says that Diana would never have thought of such an idea and that it is unjust to blame Diana.

5. In the last sentence of this chapter, Anne says, "It's splendid to find out there are so many of them in the world." What is she talking about, and who is her new one? Anne is talking about kindred spirits. Her new kindred spirit is Miss Josephine Barry, who fully accepts Anne's apology and is charmed into extending her visit to the Barrys.

Enrichment

1. Matthew "puts his oar in" and argues in Anne's favor in this chapter. Write a short paper detailing the different roles Matthew and Marilla take in raising Anne. What is Matthew's major role, and why does he interfere in this instance? Matthew's major role in raising Anne is in showing her unconditional love. Marilla takes on the role of training Anne, instructing her morally, and disciplining her. Matthew is empathetic to Anne's suffering, so he feels for her when she is faced with the possibility of being left out of an event her friends are going to. He responds to Anne's feelings while Marilla is motivated by providing for Anne's physical and moral well-being.

Expressions for Discussion

1. *"Only don't say I didn't warn you if he burns Green Gables down or puts strychnine in the well—"*
   a. Who said it? Mrs. Lynde
   b. Who is going to burn down Green Gables or poison the Cuthberts? the child the Cuthberts are adopting

2. *"I'm not in the depths of despair this morning. I never can be in the morning."*
   a. Why was Anne in "the depths of despair" the previous night? She found out that the Cuthberts wanted a boy, not her.

3. *"My life is a perfect graveyard of buried hopes."*
   a. What is the buried hope Anne is talking about? that her hair will turn a different color when she grows up

4. *"I guess it doesn't matter what a person's name is as long as he behaves himself."*
   a. Who said it? Marilla
   b. What does Anne wish her name were? Cordelia

5. *"I've been thinking over the idea until I've got kind of used to it. It seems a sort of duty."*
   a. Who said it? Marilla
   b. What is the idea she has been thinking over? keeping Anne to raise

6. *"Oh, Miss—Marilla, how much you miss!"*
   a. What is Marilla missing? using her imagination

7. *"You can shut me up in a dark, damp dungeon inhabited by snakes and toads and feed me only on bread and water and I shall not complain."*
   a. How can Anne get out of the dungeon? by apologizing to Mrs. Lynde

8. *"Well, they didn't pick you for your looks, that's sure and certain."*
   a. Who said it? Mrs. Lynde

9. *"But don't be too hard on her, Marilla. Recollect she hasn't ever had anyone to teach her right."*
   a. Who said it? Matthew

10. *"When did you ever hear of me starving people into good behavior?"*
    a. Who said it? Marilla

11. *"I'll imagine that I like them."*
    a. What is Anne going to imagine that she likes? the dresses Marilla made her that don't have puffed sleeves

12. *"I am well in body although considerably rumpled up in spirit, thank you, ma'am."*
    a. Who said it? Anne
    b. Who is she speaking to? Mrs. Barry
    c. Why is she rumpled up in spirit? She is afraid that Diana won't like her.

13. *"I have to furnish most of the imagination, but I'm well able to do that."*

a. Who does Anne have to furnish most of the imagination for? Diana

14. *"I never saw such an infatuated man. The more she talks and the odder the things she says, the more he's delighted evidently."*

a. Who said it? Marilla

b. Who is delighted by Anne's talk? Matthew

15. *"You'll feel remorse of conscience some day, I expect, for breaking it, Marilla, but I forgive you."*

a. What has Marilla broken? Anne's heart

b. How did she break it? by telling Anne she couldn't go to the picnic

16. *"Marilla, that is the first compliment I have ever had in my life and you can't imagine what a strange feeling it gave me."*

a. What is the compliment Anne received? Prissy Andrews told Anne she has a pretty nose.

17. *"The iron has entered into my soul, Diana."*

a. What has caused the iron to enter into Anne's soul?

Mr. Phillips humiliated Anne and spelled her name without an *e*.

18. *"The stars in their courses fight against me, Marilla."*

a. How are the stars fighting against Anne? Anne has made Diana drunk so they are parted forever.

19. *"... you will cover my life with a dark cloud of woe."*

a. Who is covering Anne's life with a dark cloud of woe? Mrs. Barry

20. *"Please see that it is buried with me, for I don't believe I'll live very long."*

a. What is to go into Anne's grave with her? a lock of Diana's hair

21. *"There is no scope for imagination in it at all. Mr. Phillips says I'm the worst dunce he ever saw at it."*

a. What is Anne a dunce at that leaves no scope for imagination? geometry

22. *"She seems to have a skill and presence of mind perfectly wonderful in a child of her age."*

a. Who said it? the doctor

b. What has Anne accomplished that proves her skill and presence of mind? She has saved Minnie May's life.

23. *"I cannot tie myself down to anything so unromantic as dish-washing at this thrilling moment."*

a. What is Anne's thrilling moment? Mrs. Barry has forgiven Anne and will let her and Diana be friends again.

24. *"I'm Anne of Green Gables, and I've come to confess, if you please."*

a. What is Anne's confession? It was her idea that she and Diana leap into the bed with Miss Barry.

25. *"... You seem like an interesting lady, and you might even be a kindred spirit although you don't look very much like it."*

a. Who might be Anne's new kindred spirit? Miss Josephine Barry

Who Am I?

1. Matthew and Marilla Cuthbert owners of Green Gables / adoptive parents of Anne
2. Mrs. Rachel Lynde the Cuthberts' nosy neighbor
3. Cordelia Anne's preferred name
4. Mrs. Thomas scrubwoman who took Anne in when her parents died
5. Katie Maurice and Violetta Anne's imaginary friends
6. Diana Barry Anne's bosom friend
7. Mr. Phillips the school teacher at Avonlea
8. Gilbert Blythe Anne's schoolmate and academic rival
9. Minnie May Diana's little sister who gets croup
10. Miss Josephine Barry Diana's aunt

Short Answer

1. Where is Avonlea located? Nova Scotia, in Canada
2. What is the relationship between Matthew and Marilla? brother and sister
3. Of what is Matthew mortally afraid? women and girls
4. Who does Anne think might marry her even though she's homely? a foreign missionary
5. Where is Anne's bedroom located? in the east gable room
6. Who first decides that it might be a good idea to keep Anne? Matthew
7. Who has all the authority in Anne's raising? Marilla
8. Why doesn't Anne care about God? He gave her red hair.
9. What is Anne's chief shortcoming? her daydreaming
10. What is the one thing Anne could never endure in a bosom friend? red hair
11. What is the serious disposition Marilla discovers about Anne? her bad temper
12. Who convinces Anne to apologize to Mrs. Lynde? Matthew
13. How does Anne's apology become a triumph? She turns it into a performance.
14. What is the most exciting thing about the church picnic? ice cream
15. What possession of Marilla's does Anne get the blame for losing? her amethyst brooch
16. What was Marilla's first mistake in blaming Anne for the loss? Anne has never lied to her before, so she should have trusted her not to lie.
17. How does Gilbert make an enemy of Anne? by calling her "Carrots"

18. What happens to Marilla's pudding sauce? Anne forgets to cover it and a mouse drowns in it.

19. Why does Mrs. Barry forbid the friendship of Anne and Diana? Anne gets Diana drunk by accident.

20. Where does Anne meet her Waterloo? in geometry

21. Why does Mrs. Barry forgive Anne? Anne saves Minnie May's life one night.

22. Who do Anne and Diana discover in Mrs. Barry's spare bedroom? Miss Josephine Barry

Comprehension Questions

1. Matthew quickly becomes convinced that he and Marilla should keep Anne. What are his reasons for this decision? Matthew is charmed with Anne. Her frankness and open-hearted way of dealing with him puts him at ease immediately. He comes to see that even though he and Marilla were adopting a boy to help them on the farm, Anne needs them. She needs to be loved, and Matthew quickly comes to the realization that he and Marilla can make a lasting difference in a child's life.

2. Marilla tells Matthew, "When I fail it'll be time enough to put your oar in." What does this statement mean? The analogy here is of Matthew and Marilla in a boat. Marilla will steer and control the boat with her oar, but Matthew won't even have his oar in the water until given permission by Marilla. Anne is the boat being steered. Marilla is taking control of raising Anne. Matthew will only be allowed to interfere when Marilla needs his help and gives him permission.

3. Anne "heaps coals of fire" on Mrs. Barry's head. What does it mean to heap coals of fire on someone's head? Anne heaps coals of fire on Mrs. Barry's head by totally forgiving her even though Mrs. Barry was unwilling to do the same for Anne when she got Diana drunk. If you are forgiving and consistently nice in the face of being mistreated by others, you prove yourself to be a person of moral strength and character. As Paul says in Romans 12:21, you are overcoming evil with good.

Mastery Word List

aesthetic	**arduous**	**deft**	**deprecate**
diligent	**estrange**	**irreverent**	**ostentation**
penitent	**resolute**	**staunch**	**sublime**
superfluous	**tempestuous**	**vivacious**	

Synonym Substitution

Write a few good synonyms or a phrase in the blank to replace the highlighted word.

1. Thank you for the pie, it was **sublime**. heavenly, glorious, splendid
2. The math problem was proving quite **arduous**, so I asked for help. difficult, burdensome
3. **Penitence** is required before forgiveness can be requested. remorseful, repentant
4. Everyone marvelled at how **deftly** he was able to get over the wall. skillfully, nimbly
5. "I hope it will not be **irreverent** of me to say, that if it be profitable that God would reveal his will to others, on a point so connected with my duty, it might be supposed he would reveal it directly to me." - Abraham Lincoln insulting, rude, discourteous, offensive
6. Her anger was **tempestuous** when she didn't get her way. wild, uncontrollable, furious
7. "It is the character of a brave and **resolute** man not to be ruffled by adversity and not to desert his post." - Cicero resolved, determined, tenacious, bold
8. Their **diligent** work paid off in the end. careful, attentive, steady, focused
9. The man waved **superfluously** even after the car had passed. unnecessarily, needlessly
10. "What are you doing?" she said **deprecatingly**. disapprovingly, deploringly
11. She couldn't remember what he said because his **ostentatious** bow tie had distracted her. showy, flamboyant, pretentious
12. Although the house was lovely on the inside, the exterior lacked any **aesthetic** value. artistic, tasteful, beautiful
13. The rude manager was **estranged** from his fellow workmen. alienated, separated
14. What he lacked in skill he made up for in **vivacity**. energy, enthusiasm, liveliness
15. There is nothing more valuable than a **staunch** friend. trustworthy, faithful

Mastery Substitution

Use a word from the Mastery Word List to replace the highlighted word or phrase.
You may have to change the form of the word to fit the sentence.

1. He began the meeting by **expressing disapproval of** the choice of decorations. deprecating
2. The men fought **faithfully** against the injustice of the king. staunchly
3. His refusal to shower had resulted in his being **alienated** by his classmates. estranged
4. After defeating her siblings in the game, she performed an **unnecessary** dance. superfluous
5. **Careful work** is required for mastering any skill. diligence
6. It would be **heavenly** to no longer have any homework. sublime
7. Cleaning your room is probably not as **exhausting** as you make it out to be. arduous
8. Her **lively** personality brightened up the room. vivacious
9. **In terms of beauty**, that piece of music has no equal. aesthetically
10. He was fearless as he set sail on the **stormy** seas. tempestuous
11. Mom is, sadly, **unyielding** when it comes to our bedtime. resolute
12. It is important as a politician to be **highly skilled** in avoiding answering questions. deft
13. Even if you disagree with the king, it does not mean you can be **disrespectful**. irreverent
14. When he saw the broken glass he was immediately **full of grief** about his mistake. penitent
15. The king paraded **in a boastful manner** through the city on his chariot of gold. ostentatiously

Implementation

Use at least eight of the words from the Mastery Word List in a paragraph of your own.

Reading Notes

Haunted Wood	Anne's name for the gloomy spruce wood over the brook
Victoria Island	Anne's name for the island with two maple trees surrounded by the brook
Silas Sloane	owns the land where the children gather the blooming Mayflowers
Charlie Sloane	one of Anne's classmates; his grandmother claims to have seen a ghost

Vocabulary

Write the meaning of each bold word or phrase.

1. the beautiful, **capricious***, reluctant Canadian spring adj. unpredictable; fickle
2. personality that seemed to **pervade** it v. to spread throughout, to permeate
3. with eyes **limpid** with sympathy. adj. clear; transparent
4. Oh, we have imagined the most **harrowing** things. adj. extremely distressing
5. I won't **countenance** any such doings. (special use as verb) to support; to approve
6. But Marilla was **inexorable**. adj. unable to be persuaded, relentless

*Look up "capricious" in the dictionary, and write out the complete definition, the alternate forms, and 2-3 synonyms. adj. given to a whimsical or fickle mind, unpredictable

alternate forms: capriciously - adv. capriciousness - n.

synonyms: erratic, unstable, unreliable, flighty, impulsive, fickle

Expressions for Discussion

1. *"I can't tell you the person's name because I have vowed never to let it cross my lips."* - Anne
   Whose name will never cross Anne's lips? *Gilbert's*
2. *"There's such a lot of different Annes in me. I sometimes think that is why I'm such a troublesome person. If I was just the one Anne it would be ever so much more comfortable, but then it wouldn't be half so interesting."* - Anne
3. *"You seem to have got on fairly well and made fewer mistakes than usual."* - Marilla
   What are the mistakes Anne did make? *starching Matthew's handkerchiefs and burning the pie in the oven*
4. *"… I felt instinctively that there was something missing on the dinner table."* - Anne
   What was missing? *the pie Anne left in the oven*
   Why did the pie burn? *Anne was imagining herself as an enchanted princess being rescued from a tower by a knight and forgot the pie.*
5. *"What would you feel like if a white thing did snatch me up and carry me off?"* - Anne
   To whom is Anne speaking? *Marilla*
   What is Marilla's response? *"I'll risk it."*
6. *"I'll cure you of imagining ghosts into places."* - Marilla

Comprehension Questions

Answer the following in complete sentences.

1. What does Anne think Mayflowers are? Anne thinks that mayflowers may be the souls of the flowers that died the previous summer and that this is their heaven.

2. How has the atmosphere in Anne's gable bedroom changed since her arrival at Green Gables a year ago? Anne's gable room is physically unchanged, but the character of the room is now full of Anne's vitality and personality. "It was as if all the dreams, sleeping and waking, of its vivid occupant had taken a visible although immaterial form and had tapestried the bare room with splendid filmy tissues of rainbow and moonshine."

3. How does Marilla reply to Anne's question, "Are you sorry you kept me, Marilla?" What are Marilla's inner feelings that she doesn't share with Anne? Marilla says that she isn't sorry that she kept Anne, but she doesn't tell Anne that she doesn't see how she ever lived without her there. She can't imagine a life without Anne now.

4. Anne's imagination has helped her to survive her difficult life. But in this chapter we see Anne misusing her imagination. How has Anne misused her imagination, and how does Marilla cure this misuse? Anne has used her imagination to convince herself that the woods between her house and Diana's house are haunted. Marilla has no tolerance with this and sets out to cure Anne of the overuse of her imagination by making her go through the woods at night on an errand for her.

Enrichment

1. Copy Anne's description of the Haunted Wood, beginning with the sentence, "A haunted wood is so very romantic, Marilla." ______________________________

2. Draw the Haunted Wood and Victoria Island.

"... it was really providential that Mrs. Allan was a kindred spirit."

Reading Notes

Mr. Allan	Avonlea's new minister
Mrs. Allan	the minister's wife; young and beautiful
Ruby Gillis	one of Anne's classmates; sentimental over Mr. Phillips' departure
Jane Andrews	one of Anne's classmates; plain and sensible
anodyne liniment	medicinal liquid used to soothe and relieve pain

Vocabulary

Write the meaning of each bold word or phrase.

1. I had a **presentiment** that it would be needed. n. a vague expectation; premonition; omen
2. **actuated** by any motive save her avowed one v. caused to move
3. every year of his **sojourn**. n. visit; stopover
4. Marilla was determined not to be **eclipsed***v. deprived of prominence; surpassed
5. in case the minister is **dyspeptic** adj. subject to indigestion
6. having been **inveigled** into the party v. persuaded with cunning, enticed

*Look up "eclipse" in the dictionary, and write out the complete definition, the alternate forms, and 2-3 synonyms. n. & v. n. 1. the event during which a planetary object (i.e., the moon) comes between the sun and another planetary object (i.e., Earth) 2. a fall into obscurity or disuse; a decline v. 1. to obscure light 2. to deprive of importance; to surpass *alt. forms:* eclipser - n. *v. synonyms:* 1. conceal, hide, obscure 2. surpass, outshine, overshadow

Expressions for Discussion

1. *"But one can't feel quite in the depths of despair with two months vacation before them ..."* - Anne
What event almost put Anne into "the depths of despair"? *the departure of Mr. Phillips from the Avonlea school*
2. *"She said right away she didn't think it was fair for the teacher to ask all the questions, and you know, Marilla, that is exactly what I've always thought."* - Anne
About whom is Anne talking? *Mrs. Allan*
3. *"I wish I had dimples in my cheeks, Marilla ... If I had perhaps I could influence people for good."* - Anne Who does have dimples in her cheeks? *Mrs. Allan*
4. *"I never knew before that religion was such a cheerful thing. I always thought it was kind of melancholy."* - Anne
5. *"Oh, of course he's good, but he doesn't seem to get any comfort out of it. If I could be good I'd dance and sing all day because I was glad of it."* - Anne
Who is the melancholy Christian Anne is speaking of? *Superintendent Bell*
6. *"Oh, no, it takes me to make such a mistake."* - Anne
What is Anne's mistake this time? *flavoring a cake with anodyne liniment*
7. *"Marilla, isn't it nice to think that tomorrow is a new day with no mistakes in it yet?"* - Anne

Comprehension Questions

Answer the following in complete sentences.

1. In the first sentence of this chapter, Anne says, "There is nothing but meetings and partings in this world." Who departs from Anne's life, and who enters it? Mr. Phillips departs from Anne's life when his position as Avonlea school teacher ends, and Mrs. Allan, the new minister's wife, enters Anne's life.

2. Why does Anne approve of Mr. Allan? Why does Mrs. Lynde approve of Mr. Allan? Anne says that Mr. Allan had an interesting sermon and prayed as if he meant it, not just because he is in the habit of it. Mrs. Lynde says Mr. Allan isn't perfect but he has sound theology, she knows his wife's people, who are respectable and good housekeepers, and that sound doctrine and good housekeeping make an ideal combination for success.

3. The author says that Anne "was not entirely guiltless of the wisdom of the serpent" when she convinced Marilla to let her decorate the tea table. What does this refer to, and how does Anne use a serpent's wisdom to get her way? The "wisdom of the serpent" refers to the story of Adam and Eve and the serpent who convinced Eve to disobey God. Anne used conniving wisdom when she convinced Marilla to let her decorate the tea table by telling her that Mrs. Barry had her table decorated. Anne knew that Marilla wouldn't want Mrs. Barry to outdo her, so this was a clever plan that enabled Anne to get her way.

4. Who is responsible for Anne's ruined cake? What other incident does this remind you of? Marilla is responsible for the ruined cake because she put anodyne liniment into an empty vanilla bottle and did not tell Anne. This is similar to the time Anne got Diana drunk because Marilla told her to look in the wrong place for the raspberry cordial.

5. What does Anne find encouraging about the mistakes she makes? Anne thinks that there must be a limit to the number of mistakes one person can make, and once Anne gets to the end of them, she won't make any more mistakes.

Enrichment

1. This chapter is full of "Mrs. Lynde sayings." Go back through the chapter and make a list of the maxims Mrs. Lynde is credited with.

For Anne to take things calmly would have been to change her nature.

Reading Notes

manse	a minister's house; Mr. and Mrs. Allan's home
Lauretta Bradley	the other girl invited to tea; from the White Sands Sunday school

Vocabulary

Write the meaning of each bold word or phrase.

1. like a wind-blown **sprite** n. elf or fairy
2. her model little girl of **demure** manners adj. quiet; shy; reserved
3. demure manners and prim **deportment**. n. manners; behavior
4. loving its strange, **sonorous**, haunting rhythm adj. having a full, rich sound
5. a very sound and **pithy*** piece of advice. adj. short and forceful
6. she looked just like a **seraph**. n. angel

*Look up "pithy" in the dictionary, and write out the complete definition, the alternate forms, and 2-3 synonyms. adj. short or condensed but full of meaning
alternate forms: pithily - adv. pithiness - n.
synonyms: terse, forceful, condensed

Expressions for Discussion

1. *"Oh, Marilla, there is something in me today that makes me just love everybody I see."* - Anne
   What is special about this day? *Anne is going to tea at the manse.*
2. *"I believe I could be a model child if I were just invited out to tea every day."* - Anne
   To whom is she speaking? *Marilla*
3. *"I really think I'd like to be a minister's wife when I grow up, Marilla. A minister mightn't mind my red hair because he wouldn't be thinking of such worldly things."* - Anne
4. *"Mrs. Lynde says I'm full of original sin."* - Anne
5. *"You know there are some people, like Matthew and Mrs. Allan, that you can love right off without any trouble. And there are others, like Mrs. Lynde, that you have to try very hard to love."* - Anne
6. *"I really don't see how I'm going to live through the two weeks before school begins, I'm so impatient to see her."* - Anne
   Who is Anne impatient to see? *her new female teacher*

Comprehension Questions

Answer the following in complete sentences.

1. What does Marilla feel is her duty to Anne? What doesn't she admit to herself? Marilla worries that Anne's emotions are so strong that she will always be subject to great hurt in life. So Marilla has made it her duty to train Anne into tranquil, calm feelings so that she would be spared from undue worry and hurt. Marilla doesn't admit to herself that she really prefers Anne as she is and would be sorry if she actually succeeded in calming Anne's strong emotional energy and vivacity.Marilla doesn't understand that Anne's capacity for great feeling is balanced so that her ability to delight in the good more than compensates for the depths of despair Anne is plunged into when she is disappointed by the hardships in life.

2. What does Anne think would make her into a model child? Anne thinks that if she were invited out to tea every day, she could be a model child.

3. What is Marilla's "sound and pithy" advice? Rewrite this advice in your own words. When Anne is concerned about her behavior at Mrs. Allan's tea party, Marilla tells her that she is thinking too much about herself and she would be better served to think about suiting her behavior to what would be "nicest and most agreeable" for Mrs. Allan.

4. Why does Anne think she could never be a minister's wife? Anne thinks she could never be a minister's wife because one would have to be naturally good and she will never be that. She thinks that no matter how hard she tries to be good, she will never succeed at it like she would if she were naturally good.

Enrichment

1. Add to your list of Mrs. Lynde sayings. You should find at least two in this chapter.
   I'm full of original sin; they've never had a female teacher in Avonlea before and she thinks it is a dangerous innovation.

2. The author refers to Anne as being "spirit and fire and dew." This phrase comes directly from a poem by Robert Browning called "Evelyn Hope." Read this poem (located in the Appendix). What is the theme of the poem?
   This poem is about the death of a sixteen-year-old girl named Evelyn Hope. It is written by one who loved her and will not forget her. It is the kind of sad, melancholy poem Anne would have been drawn to.

Reading Notes

Carrie Sloane one of Anne's classmates; starts the series of dares among the girls

Josie Pye one of Anne's classmates; disliked by many; dares Anne to walk the ridge-pole

Vocabulary

Write the meaning of each bold word or phrase.

1. **albeit** in mortal dread ______ prep. although
2. to the **discomfiture** of the aforesaid Carrie Sloane. n. disappointment; frustration
3. a natural and inborn gift, duly **cultivated** ______ v. intentionally improved or developed
4. "Don't you do it, Anne," **entreated*** Diana. ______ v. pleaded; begged
5. on that **precarious*** footing ______ adj. unstable; insecure
6. I think I am **rendered** unconscious. ______ v. made

*Look up the following words in the dictionary, and write out the complete definition, the alternate forms, and 2-3 synonyms for each word.

entreat: v. to ask earnestly
alternate forms: entreatingly - adv.
synonyms: plead, beg

precarious: adj. 1. unstable, insecure 2. uncertain, dependent on chance
alternate forms: precariously - adv. precariousness - n.
synonyms: perilous, unsteady, shaky, doubtful, unpredictable

Expressions for Discussion

1. *"I must do it. My honor is at stake. ... If I am killed you are to have my pearl bead ring."* - Anne
   Who is to get Anne's pearl bead ring if she is killed? *Diana*
2. *"I expect I have sprained my ankle. But, Marilla, I might have broken my neck. Let us look on the bright side of things."* - Anne
3. *"... The thought that it is all my own fault is what makes it so hard. If I could blame it on anybody I would feel so much better."* - Anne
4. *"Oh, I am an afflicted mortal."* - Anne
   Why is Anne afflicted? *She has to miss school for weeks, so she won't meet the new teacher and will get behind Gilbert in school.*
5. *"You're an unlucky child, there's no doubt about that."* - Marilla

6. *"If I had been killed she would have had to carry a dark burden of remorse all her life."* - Anne
Who would have a dark burden to carry if Anne had died? Josie Pye
Why? Josie is the person who dared Anne to walk the ridge-pole.

7. *"There's one thing plain to be seen, Anne, and that is that your fall off the Barry roof hasn't injured your tongue at all."* - Marilla

Comprehension Questions

Answer the following in complete sentences.

1. Which one of Anne's friends is most relieved that Anne isn't killed falling from the ridge-pole? Why? Josie Pye is most relieved that Anne isn't killed because she is the one who dared Anne to walk the ridge-pole, and as Anne says, "If I had been killed she would have had to carry a dark burden of remorse all her life."
2. What is Marilla's revelation at the news of Anne's injury? Marilla realizes that Anne is dearer to her than anything on earth. Her revelation is that she loves Anne as a daughter.
3. What wish does Anne have granted to her in this chapter? Anne has always wished she could faint, and that wish is granted when she is injured.
4. What is the "broad hint" Anne gives to Superintendent Bell when he comes to visit her? What is Mrs. Lynde's hope for Anne when she visits? Anne has decided that Superintendent Bell is not insincere when he prays, but he has gotten into the habit of saying prayers as if he doesn't mean them. So Anne gives him a broad hint that he should make his prayers interesting by telling him that she strives to make her own private prayers interesting.
5. Name the new activities Miss Stacy introduces to the Avonlea school. Miss Stacy has introduced recitations, field days outside to study nature, and physical culture exercises into the curriculum at the Avonlea school.

Enrichment

1. In this chapter Anne comes to grief in an "affair of honor." What is an affair of honor, and why does offended honor often cause humans to risk lives or act foolishly?
   An affair of honor is a dispute over someone's good reputation or esteem. Humans will often take foolish risks if someone has questioned their honor because that is a question of character, and one's character is important enough to defend. Josie questions Anne's integrity by doubting her claim that she knows someone who could walk a ridge-pole and that she herself is capable of that. Anne feels the need to defend her reputation for honesty.

Reading Notes

Miss Stacy Anne's new teacher; bright, young, and sympathetic; beloved by students

Vocabulary

Write the meaning of each bold word or phrase.

1. the ferns were **sear** and brown adj. scorched or withered
2. I feel **instinctively** that she's spelling it adv. in a manner known or felt without having to learn; intuitively
3. physical culture **contortions** paled n. twistings, things in a twisted state
4. for the **laudable** purpose of helping adj. praiseworthy; commendable
5. And we're to have a **tableau** n. a frozen scene (usually from history or literature)
6. conflicts between **inclination** and said duty. n. leaning; partiality

Expressions for Discussion

1. *"When she pronounces my name I feel* instinctively *that she's spelling it with an* e.*"* - Anne
   Who instinctively pronounces Anne's name with an *e*? *Miss Stacy*
2. *"I know I won't be able to make your blood run cold."* - Anne
   Who's blood will Anne try to make run cold? *Matthew's*
3. *"… I assure you it is a humbling reflection."* - Anne
   What is humbling to Anne? *her struggle with geometry*
4. *"Oh, I would dearly love to be remarkable."* - Anne
5. *"Fudge! There's precious little patriotism in the thoughts of any of you. All you want is a good time."* - Marilla
   What is Marilla fussing about? *the idea of a concert put on by the Avonlea school*
6. *"Don't be alarmed if you hear me groaning."* - Anne
   Why will Anne be groaning? *She needs to groan in one of her recitations.*
7. *"You are simply good for nothing just now with your head stuffed full of dialogues and groans and tableaux."* - Marilla
8. *"Well, now, I reckon it's going to be a pretty good concert. And I expect you'll do your part fine."* - Matthew

Comprehension Questions

Answer the following in complete sentences.

1. What is Miss Stacy's newest project? What is Marilla's opinion about this project? Miss Stacy's newest project is for the Avonlea students to perform in a concert on Christmas night for the purpose of earning money for a new schoolhouse flag. Marilla thinks this is a foolish idea that will fill the students' heads with nonsense. She thinks their time would be better spent on their lessons. She is afraid that a concert will make the students vain and forward.

2. What is Anne's part in this project? Anne is in two dialogues, she has two recitations, and she is in a tableau.

3. Why does Anne go to the yard to sit with Matthew? Anne takes refuge with Matthew when Marilla is so critical of the concert. She knows that Matthew will let her talk as much as she likes about the concert and he will be an appreciative and sympathetic listener.

4. What is Matthew thankful for? Why? Matthew is thankful that Marilla has taken on the role of raising Anne so that Matthew can just relax and be Anne's friend. Since he doesn't have the duty of teaching and disciplining her, he is free to spoil her.

5. Explain the last sentence in this chapter: "… a little 'appreciation' sometimes does quite as much good as all the conscientious 'bringing up' in the world." Teaching and disciplining are necessary in child-rearing, but children also need to have love and to be appreciated as people. Matthew realized early on that Anne would respond positively to being loved and appreciated, and he takes that responsibility in her upbringing. The different kinds of care that Anne receives from both Matthew and Marilla are important in shaping her into the person she is becoming.

Enrichment

1. Reread the second paragraph in this chapter. What kind of teacher is Miss Stacy? How is she a good influence for Anne? Who is the teacher who has been most influential in your life? How was this teacher an inspiration to you?

Reading Notes

bootjack	a forked device for holding a boot secure while the foot is being withdrawn
Samuel Lawson	owns the store where Matthew goes to buy Anne's dress
William Blair	owns another store, where the Cuthberts usually shop
Miss Harris	the lady clerk at Lawson's store who helps Matthew
gloria	a silk, wool, cotton, or nylon fabric

Vocabulary

Write the meaning of each bold word or phrase.

1. Anne and a **bevy** of her schoolmates n. group
2. He had **recourse** to his pipe n. a source of help; refuge
3. Probably some wise **inscrutable*** motive adj. mysterious; incomprehensible
4. an **unwarranted** putting in of his oar adj. groundless; unjustified
5. After much **cogitation** n. consideration; serious thought
6. briskly and **ingratiatingly** adv. in a pleasing or flattering manner

*Look up "inscrutable" in the dictionary, and write out the complete definition, the alternate forms, and 2-3 synonyms. adj. difficult or impossible to comprehend

alternate forms: inscrutability - n. inscrutableness - n. inscrutably - adv.

synonyms: mysterious, incomprehensible

Expressions for Discussion

1. *"That man is waking up after being asleep for over sixty years."* - Mrs. Lynde
2. *"I knew he was up to some foolishness."* - Marilla
   Who is up to foolishness? *Matthew* What is the foolishness? *having a fashionable dress made for Anne*
3. *"Breakfast seems so commonplace at such an exciting moment."* - Anne
   What is the exciting moment? *Anne receiving her Christmas present from Matthew*
4. *"Then I thought of my lovely puffed sleeves and took courage. I knew that I must live up to those sleeves, Diana."* - Anne
   What did Anne do to live up to her sleeves? *She gave a great performance in the concert.*
5. *"Did I groan all right?"* - Anne
   To whom is Anne speaking? *Diana* What was Diana's response? *"Yes, indeed, you groaned lovely."*
6. *"Anne, I do think it's awful mean the way you treat Gil."* - Diana
7. *"Things like that are all the better for lots of thinking over."* - Matthew
   What is Matthew thinking over? *further schooling for Anne after she leaves Avonlea school*

Comprehension Questions

Answer the following in complete sentences.

1. What is the difference between Anne and her friends that Matthew discovers? What does Matthew think Marilla would say is the difference between Anne and her friends? Matthew discovers that Anne is not dressed like her friends. Anne is dressed plainly and soberly in dark colors, while her friends are dressed in gay, bright colors with fashionable puffed sleeves. Matthew feels that if he discusses this with Marilla, she will say that the only difference between Anne and her friends is that Anne never keeps her tongue quiet and the other girls can.

2. What is Mrs. Lynde's criticism of Marilla's raising of Anne? Rachel Lynde thinks that Marilla is trying to raise Anne according to a particular method or idea she has in her head about the proper way to raise children, but Rachel believes that "flesh and blood don't come under the head of arithmetic" and that while Marilla is trying to cultivate humility in Anne by dressing her plainly, she is more likely cultivating envy and discontent.

3. What is Marilla's opinion of puffed sleeves? Marilla thinks that puffed sleeves are silly and that since they keep getting bigger and bigger as the styles change, by next year anybody who wears them will have to go through doors sideways.

4. What does Aunt Josephine give Anne for Christmas? Why does Diana consider this a blessing? Aunt Josephine gives Anne a dainty pair of kid slippers with beaded toes, satin bows, and glistening buckles. Diana considers this a blessing because now Anne will not have to borrow Ruby's slippers for the concert. Ruby's slippers are two sizes too big for Anne, and Diana feels it would be awful to hear a fairy shuffling, as Anne would have done in slippers that were too large for her.

5. Marilla and Matthew are both proud of Anne's performance at the concert. What is the difference in the way they handle their pride in Anne? Matthew freely tells Anne that he is proud of her, but Marilla says that even though she is proud of Anne, she is not going to tell her. This is another example of the different ideas Matthew and Marilla have about raising a child. Again, Matthew is consistent in his belief that love and appreciation are at least as influential as rule-making and imparting morals when it comes to training a child into obedience and strength of character.

Enrichment

1. Read Henry Glassford Bell's "Mary, Queen of Scots" (located in the Appendix). Memorize the last two stanzas and recite them to an audience. Can you make your audience's blood "run cold"?

"I think this story-writing business is the foolishest yet."

Reading Notes

Moody Spurgeon one of Anne's classmates; fought with Charlie Sloane
Alice Bell Anne's sixteen-year-old classmate who wears her hair up
Rosamond Montmorency Anne's pen name

Vocabulary

Write the meaning of each bold word or phrase.

1. who had quarrelled over a point of **precedence** n. priority in time, order, or importance
2. it **behooved** them to be observant. v. required; compelled
3. not to look virtuously **complacent** adj. self-satisfied; smug
4. their funeral was most **imposing** adj. impressive in appearance, formidable
5. Ruby Gillis **opined** that their admission v. held or expressed as an opinion
6. We each write under a **nom de plume**. n. pen name; pseudonym

Expressions for Discussion

1. *"... I don't believe I'd really want to be a sensible person, because they are so unromantic."* - Anne
   To whom is Anne speaking? *Diana*
   Who does Anne think is a sensible person? *Marilla*
   Who thinks Anne will never be a sensible person? *Mrs. Lynde*
2. *"Mrs. Allan says we should never make uncharitable speeches; but they do slip out so often before you think, don't they?"* - Anne
3. *"I'm afraid I think too much about my nose ever since I heard that compliment about it long ago. It really is a great comfort to me."* - Anne
4. *"It's so much more romantic to end a story up with a funeral than a wedding."* - Anne
5. *"We are going to keep them all sacredly and have them to read to our descendants."* - Anne
   What are Anne and her friends going to have to read to their descendants? *the stories they are writing*
6. *"Is it very wicked of me, Marilla, to feel encouraged when I hear that other people have been bad and mischievous?"* - Anne
   Who has made Anne feel encouraged? *Mrs. Allan*

Comprehension Questions

Answer the following in complete sentences.

1. This chapter marks a turning point in Anne's life. What is that turning point? Anne turns thirteen. She is becoming a young lady.
2. What is Anne's "besetting sin"? What does Mrs. Lynde say Mr. Allan's besetting sin is? Anne's "besetting sin" is her imagination that is responsible for her forgetting her duties. Mrs. Lynde says that Mr. Allan's besetting sin is that he thinks too much of his wife. A minister should not "set his affections so much on a mortal being," according to Mrs. Lynde.
3. Contrast the different responses Marilla and Matthew have to Anne's story when she reads it to them. Which response does Anne favor? Marilla says that Anne's story is "stuff and nonsense," but Matthew says it is fine. Anne prefers Matthew's response.
4. How does Diana—who has a limited imagination, according to Anne—solve the problem of ending her stories? Diana doesn't know what to do with her characters, so she kills them off to get rid of them. Anne believes Diana has too many murders in her stories.
5. What is Marilla's opinion of the story club? How does Anne defend her club? Marilla thinks the story club is foolish and will encourage the girls to get a pack of nonsense into their heads and waste time that would be better spent on their studies.
6. Why is Anne puzzled over Aunt Josephine's reaction to the girls' stories? Aunt Josephine is highly amused at the melodrama in the story club stories, but Anne sees nothing humorous in the sad, pathetic stories in which so many people die. She would expect tears, not laughter, from anyone reading them.
7. What is the moral Marilla imparts to Anne at the end of this chapter? Marilla's final moral in this chapter is, "Learn to work first and talk afterwards."

Enrichment

1. Write your own version of an Anne story. Make sure you comply with Anne's standards of imagination, drama, great emotion, and pathetic endings.
2. Find the personification in the paragraph beginning, "If I had Alice Bell's crooked nose …" In speaking of the woods in winter, Anne says, "They're so white and still, as if they were **asleep and dreaming pretty dreams**."

"Just as soon as she grows out of one freak she takes up with another."

Reading Notes

Angel Gabriel	the angel who appeared to Mary to announce the birth of Jesus
scrape	an embarrassing predicament
shingle	to cut hair short and close to the head
becoming	pleasing or attractive to the eye

Vocabulary

Write the meaning of each bold word or phrase.

1. **subjective** analysis of her thoughts and feelings adj. personal; nonobjective
2. in several little **coruscations** of glory n. flashes; sparkles
3. and more **vim** than was strictly necessary n. strength; energy
4. looked **scrutinizingly** at Anne's hair adv. with close Test; piercingly
5. I believed every word he said **implicitly***. adv. unquestioningly; without doubt
6. however his **veracity*** might be impeached n. truthfulness; honesty

*Look up the following words in the dictionary, and write out the complete definition, the alternate forms, and 2-3 synonyms for each word.

implicit: adj. 1. implied indirectly, not directly expressed 2. contained in the nature of something 3. having no reservations or doubts *alt. forms:* implicitly - adv. implicitness - n.
synonyms: 1. understood, unspoken, implied 2. inherent, intrinsic, basic 3. absolute, unquestioning

veracity/veracious: *veracity:* n. honesty, accuracy; *veracious:* adj. truthful
alternate forms: veraciously - adv. veraciousness - n.
synonyms: truth, honesty, accuracy, precision

Expressions for Discussion

1. *"But I'm bringing her up and not Rachel Lynde, who'd pick faults in the Angel Gabriel himself if he lived in Avonlea."* - Marilla
2. *"... Anne's a great hand at explaining."* - Matthew
   What does Anne need to explain? *why she didn't have tea ready when Marilla got home*
3. *"Little things like that are of no importance now because I don't suppose I'll ever be able to go anywhere again. My career is closed."* - Anne
   What are the little things that are of no importance? *who gets head in class, who writes the best composition, and who sings in the Sunday-school choir*
4. *"I've been expecting something queer for some time. You haven't got into any scrape for over two months, and I was sure another one was due."* - Marilla

5. *"I'm going to weep all the time you're cutting it off, if it won't interfere. It seems such a tragic thing."* - Anne
6. *"It makes you feel very virtuous when you forgive people, doesn't it?"* - Anne
   Who has Anne forgiven? *Josie Pye*
   What did Josie do that needed forgiveness? *She told Anne that she looked like a scarecrow.*

Comprehension Questions

Answer the following in complete sentences.

1. What is Matthew's response to Marilla's judgment of Anne as being "disobedient or untrustworthy"? Matthew thinks Marilla should not judge Anne until she is sure Anne has disobeyed her. He wants to give Anne the benefit of the doubt until she has had an opportunity to defend herself.

2. How does Anne defend her willingness to do something "wicked" like dyeing her hair? Anne admits that dyeing her hair was a little wicked, but she feels it is worth being a little wicked in order to get rid of red hair. She is planning to be extra good to make up for it.

3. What is the penance Anne sets for herself? Anne wants to turn her mirror to the wall so she can't look at her appearance, but she commits to looking at herself every time she comes into her room and not trying to imagine away her ugly hair as a penance for being vain.

4. What is Marilla's final word on Anne's "chatter" at the end of this chapter? Marilla finally admits that she doesn't mind Anne's chatter, but has gotten used to it. She is recognizing that she likes to hear Anne's chatter.

Enrichment

1. Anne quotes from Sir Walter Scott's epic poem "Marmion" when she says to Marilla, "What a tangled web we weave when first we practice to deceive." What is the meaning of this line? How does it apply to Anne's life?

   When we begin telling lies, many times we end up having to tell more lies to cover up for our first lie. We become tangled up in deception. Anne's deception of dyeing her hair leads to her having to find a way to explain why her hair has been cut off and results in her fearing the loss of her reputation in the community. She has enmeshed herself in deception when dyeing her hair seemed like such a small offense.

"... Anne was devoured by secret regret that she had not been born in Camelot."

Reading Notes

pall to cover with a pall; a cloth covering, usually black, spread over a coffin or tomb
samite a heavy silk fabric, often interwoven with gold or silver, worn in the Middle Ages
crepe a soft thin fabric of silk, cotton, wool, or another fiber, with a crinkled surface

Vocabulary

Write the meaning of each bold word or phrase.

1. They had analysed and **parsed** it v. dissected; broken down
2. **allayed** and softened by time seemingly. v. relieved; alleviated
3. Here Ruby Gillis had **succumbed*** to hysterics v. yielded; surrendered
4. she said **haughtily** as she turned away. adv. in an arrogantly self-admiring or prideful manner
5. restored her to her **wonted** cheerfulness. adj. usual; customary
6. "I'm sure I hope so," said Marilla **sceptically***. adv. in a questioning manner; doubtingly

*Look up the following words in the dictionary, and write out the complete definition, the alternate forms, and 2-3 synonyms for each word.

succumb: v. 1. to be overcome; yield 2. to die
synonyms: yield, surrender, submit, capitulate

skeptical: adj. questioning the truth of generally accepted ideas; expressing doubt
alternate forms: skeptically - adv. skepticism - n. (sceptical - British alternate spelling)
synonyms: doubting, critical, incredulous, cynical, disbelieving

Expressions for Discussion

1. *"But it's so ridiculous to have a red-headed Elaine. ... Now, a red-haired person cannot be a lily maid."* - Anne
2. *"You don't think much about romance when you have just escaped from a watery grave."* - Anne
3. *"Anne Shirley! How on earth did you get there?"* - Gilbert
4. *"It is all my fault. I feel sure I was born under an unlucky star. Everything I do gets me or my dearest friends into a scrape."* - Anne
5. *"Will you ever have any sense, Anne?"* - Marilla
Why does Anne think she will have sense one day? *Every mistake she makes teaches her a valuable lesson, so one day she will be cured of all mistakes.*
6. *"I have come to the conclusion that it is no use trying to be romantic in Avonlea. It was probably easy enough in towered Camelot hundreds of years ago, but romance is not appreciated now."* - Anne

Comprehension Questions

Answer the following in complete sentences.

1. Describe the circumstances that result in Anne's latest scrape. Anne and her friends are reenacting Lord Tennyson's "Lancelot and Elaine" by placing Anne in a small boat on the river—as the dead Elaine of Astolat. When Anne is floating down the river, the boat begins to leak, and Anne ends up grabbing a bridge pile and holding on until she is rescued.

2. Why doesn't Anne shut her eyes when she prays to God for help? What is her prayer? Anne says that she knows that the only way God can save her is to let the boat float close enough to one of the bridge piles so she could climb onto it. She needs to keep her eyes open so she can help God help her. Her prayer is, "Dear God, please take the flat close to a pile and I'll do the rest."

3. How does Anne respond to her rescuer? How does she respond to his plea for peace between them? How does her response leave her feeling? Anne is furious that she has been rescued by Gilbert. She is scornful and frigid to him. Anne wants to respond positively to Gilbert's plea for peace, but she can't let go of the bitterness she has felt for him since he called her "Carrots," so she rejects his offer. She regrets that rejection and wants to cry over it.

4. Anne names several mistakes she has made and the shortcomings those mistakes have cured her of. List these mistakes and the shortcomings that were cured.
   The affair of the amethyst brooch cured Anne of meddling with things that didn't belong to her.
   The Haunted Wood mistake cured Anne of letting her imagination run away with her.
   The liniment cake mistake cured Anne of carelessness in cooking.
   Dyeing her hair cured Anne of vanity.
   The affair of the leaking boat cured Anne of being too romantic.

5. How does Matthew respond to Anne's conclusion that she is now cured of being too romantic? Matthew tells Anne not to give up all her romance. He says, "… a little of it is a good thing—not too much, of course—but keep a little of it, Anne, keep a little of it."

Enrichment

1. If you are not familiar with the King Arthur story of Lancelot and Elaine, find the story in a King Arthur volume and read it. Then read the excerpt from Alfred, Lord Tennyson's idyll, "Lancelot and Elaine" (located in the Appendix).

Reading Notes

Exhibition a large-scale public showing, as of art, industrial, or agricultural products

Vocabulary

Write the meaning of each bold word or phrase.

1. repeating aloud the battle **canto** n. a division of a long poem
2. rather **abashed** by the splendor adj. embarrassed, disconcerted
3. where a noted **prima donna** was to sing. n. leading female soloist in an opera
4. That sounded so **prosaic*** adj. unromantic, dull
5. thinking less about Anne's **quaint*** speeches adj. unusual, odd
6. I feel that it marks an **epoch** in my life n. noteworthy, memorable event

*Look up the following words in the dictionary, and write out the complete definition, the alternate forms, and 2-3 synonyms for each word.

prosaic: adj. 1. lacking the elegance of poetry 2. overly plain; unromantic
alternate forms: prosaically - adv. prosaicness - n.
synonyms: dull, commonplace, mediocre, bland

quaint: adj. 1. strange or odd 2. pleasingly unusual or old-fashioned
alternate forms: quaintly - adv. quaintness - n.
synonyms: strange, peculiar, eccentric, offbeat, old-fashioned, antiquated, picturesque

Expressions for Discussion

1. *"It is ever so much easier to be good if your clothes are fashionable."* - Anne
2. *"I'm trying not to imagine myself walking up the church aisle on Sunday in my new suit and cap, because I'm afraid it isn't right to imagine such things. But it just slips into my mind in spite of me."* - Anne
3. *"... She thought it was ridiculous for a Sunday-school superintendent to take a prize in pigs ... She said she would always think of it after this when he was praying so solemnly."* - Diana
4. *"... I never knew how much I really liked her until I saw her familiar face among all those strangers."* - Anne
   Whose familiar face did Anne see? *Mrs. Lynde's*
   Where did she see Mrs. Lynde? *at the Exhibition*
5. *"It's always wrong to do anything you can't tell the minister's wife. It's as good as an extra conscience to have a minister's wife for your friend."* - Anne
   What did Anne avoid doing for the sake of Mrs. Allan? *betting on the horses*

6. *"If I'd a child like Anne in the house all the time I'd be a better and happier woman."* - Miss Barry

7. *"It's been fearful lonesome here without you, and I never put in four longer days."* - Marilla

Comprehension Questions

Answer the following in complete sentences.

1. Why does Anne find herself uncomfortable in the luxury of Miss Barry's parlor? Anne feels that since everything is so splendid, there is no scope for the imagination. When one is poor, there is so much more one can imagine about.

2. Why didn't Mrs. Lynde go to the horse races? Mrs. Lynde feels that horse racing is an abomination and it is her duty as a church member to set a good example by abstaining from attending them.

3. Why does Anne decide she prefers country life to city life? Anne had a great time in the city, but she found that she missed her room in the country, knowing that the stars were shining outside and that the wind was blowing in the firs across the brook. The city is a nice place for a visit, but the country is home to Anne.

4. Describe Miss Barry's character based on the author's characterization of her in this chapter. Miss Barry is rather a selfish old lady who has never cared much for anybody but herself. She values people only as they are of service to her or amuse her. She does recognize that she would be a better person if she had a child like Anne in her life, so she is aware of her moral failings in that respect.

5. What does Anne feel is the best part of her trip to the city? Anne feels that the best part of her trip to the city is coming home.

Enrichment

1. Write a paragraph about an epoch in your life.

"... I've grown so interested in my pupils here that I found I couldn't leave them."

Reading Notes

Turk-fashion	cross-legged
Queen's	a school for training students to become teachers
chum	an intimate friend or companion

Vocabulary

Write the meaning of each bold word or phrase.

1. **refrain** from rushing impulsively ______ v. to avoid doing; to abstain
2. **tacitly** acknowledged their superiority ______ adv. in a manner that is implied without being stated, silently
3. had **evinced*** no recognition whatever ______ v. made evident, displayed
4. its last **spasmodic** flicker. ______ adj. convulsive; given to fits
5. Anne felt his **retaliatory** scorn. ______ adj. punishing; vengeful
6. Marilla Cuthbert'll live to **rue** the step she's took. ______ v. to regret

*Look up "evince" in the dictionary, and write out the complete definition, the alternate forms, and 2-3 synonyms. ______ v. to show or demonstrate clearly; to make evident

alternate forms: evincible - adj. evincive - adj.

synonyms: demonstrate, manifest, confirm, display

Expressions for Discussion

1. *"Young men are all very well in their place, but it doesn't do to drag them into everything, does it?"*
   - Anne What are Anne and Diana considering? *never marrying and being old maids together*
2. *"Of course it's a little too exciting to be proper reading for Sunday, and I only read it on weekdays."*
   - Anne What does Anne only read on weekdays? *Ben-Hur*
3. *"It's really wonderful, Marilla, what you can do when you're truly anxious to please a certain person."*
   - Anne Who is Anne anxious to please? *Miss Stacy*
   How does she please her? *by not finishing a book Miss Stacy disapproved of*
4. *"I know I talk too much, but I am really trying to overcome it, and although I say far too much, yet if you only knew how many things I want to say and don't, you'd give me some credit for it."* - Anne
   To whom is Anne speaking? *Marilla*
5. *"... I'm going to let my imagination run riot for the summer. Oh, you needn't be alarmed, Marilla. I'll only let it run riot within reasonable limits."* - Anne
6. *"... He takes them spells oftener than he used to and I'm anxious about him."* - Marilla
   To whom is Marilla speaking? *Mrs. Lynde*
   About whom is Marilla concerned? *Matthew*
7. *"I did make a mistake in judging Anne, but it weren't no wonder, for an odder, unexpecteder witch of a child there never was in this world, that's what."* - Mrs. Lynde

Comprehension Questions

Answer the following in complete sentences.

1. The author gives the reader insight into Marilla's heart in this chapter. Why does she treat Anne as she does, and what does Anne really mean to Marilla? Marilla rarely shows Anne the love that she feels for her because she feels it is sinful to set one's heart so intensely on any human creature. By being stricter and more critical of Anne, she is trying to offset the strength of feeling she has for Anne, as a kind of penance. Marilla loves Anne with a strong, deep affection.

2. What are the two wrongs Anne commits in school when she is reading *Ben-Hur* in class? First, Anne was wasting time that should have been devoted to her schoolwork, and her second wrong was in attempting to deceive Miss Stacy.

3. What are Anne's feelings for Gilbert now? What is her regret? Anne is sorry that she rejected Gilbert's plea for a truce between them because now that he is ignoring her, she finds that she cares about him. Her old resentment against him is gone. Her regret is that she has forgiven Gilbert, but she missed the opportunity to tell him and make peace with him because of her pride and stubbornness.

4. What belief does Anne believe she will have to give up after this last summer as a little girl? Anne is afraid that she will have to give up her belief in fairies in the fall when she becomes a serious, grown-up student. But she is determined to believe in fairies with her whole heart during the summer.

5. Why does Marilla miss the Aid meeting? Marilla misses the Aid meeting because Matthew had a bad spell with his heart and she was afraid to leave him.

6. How has Mrs. Lynde's opinion of Anne changed? What does she think of Anne now? Mrs. Lynde no longer thinks that Marilla made a mistake in adopting Anne. She thinks that Anne has turned out to be really smart and a great help to Marilla. She admits that she was mistaken about Anne. She also believes that Anne has turned into a pretty girl.

Enrichment

1. Add at least two "Mrs. Lynde maxims" to your list.

   We can't have things perfect in this imperfect world; Jane's father is a perfect old crank, and meaner than second skimmings; Moody Spurgeon couldn't be anything other than a minister with a name like that to live up to; Charlie Sloane won't succeed in politics because the Sloanes are all honest people, and it's only the rascals that get on in politics nowadays; if Anne keeps stretching out next year as she's done this, she'll have to put on longer skirts. She's all running to legs and eyes.

... fresh, fascinating fields of unexplored knowledge seemed to be opening out before Anne's eager eyes.

Vocabulary

Write the meaning of each bold word or phrase.

1. because I'm really bad and **unregenerate** adj. sinful; obstinately bad
2. the Queen's class **gird** up their loins v. to prepare for action; to secure one's clothes with a belt
3. for the **fray** n. a noisy fight or brawl
4. Gilbert Blythe's name was **blazoned** at the top v. announced; proclaimed
5. mindful of the Spencervale doctor's **dictum** n. a formal saying; maxim
6. almost **verging** on grown-up affairs n. bordering

Expressions for Discussion

1. *"Oh, you good old friends, I'm glad to see your honest face once more ..."* - Anne
   Who are Anne's "good old friends"? *her schoolbooks*
2. *"She does plenty of unofficial preaching as it is."* - Marilla
   Who preaches unofficially? *Mrs. Lynde*
3. *"I feel it's a great responsibility because I have only the one chance. If I don't grow up right I can't go back and begin over again."* - Anne
   To whom is Anne speaking? *Marilla*
4. *"I know I'll be able to study better because of mine. I shall have such a comfortable feeling deep down in my mind about that flounce."* - Anne
5. *"But there—men can't understand these things!"* - Marilla
   What does Marilla think Matthew can't understand? *that Anne's leaving will change everything for them, even if she can come home frequently*
6. *"I wish it was all over, Marilla. It haunts me. Sometimes I wake up in the night and wonder what I'll do if I don't pass."* - Anne
   What is Anne haunted by? *not passing the Queen's exams*

Comprehension Questions

Answer the following in complete sentences.

1. Why does Marilla lighten up and let Anne go on more outings and have more freedom outside?
   The Spencervale doctor sees Anne and sends a message to Marilla that Anne needs to stay out in the open air all summer and not read books until she gets more spring into her step. This message frightens Marilla so that she allows Anne to wander outside to her heart's content and occasionally attend social events.

2. What is Mrs. Lynde's opinion of female ministers? Who do Marilla and Anne think could be a successful female minister? Mrs. Lynde thinks the idea of women ministers is scandalous. Anne thinks that Mrs. Lynde can pray every bit as well as Superintendent Bell and could probably preach with a little practice. Marilla thinks that Mrs. Lynde could definitely preach since she does plenty of unofficial preaching as it is.

3. What troubles Anne that makes her feel she might be "bad and unregenerate"? What is Marilla's response to this concern? Anne feels desperately wicked when she is with Mrs. Lynde because she wants to do the very things Mrs. Lynde tells her not to do. She finds it an irresistible temptation to act against Mrs. Lynde's maxims. Marilla laughs and tells Anne that Rachel often has the same effect on her. She thinks that Rachel could have more influence over people if she would quit nagging them to do right.

4. What kind of teacher is Miss Stacy? How is she an inspiration to her students? Miss Stacy provides tactful, careful, broad-minded guidance to her students. She leads them to think, explore, and discover for themselves, and she encourages them to stray into new territory in their learning. She inspires them to put their brains to work, rather than depending on her to feed them answers to their questions.

5. Why does Marilla feel a sense of loss as Anne matures? How does this differ from Matthew's feelings about an older Anne? Marilla knows that when Anne leaves for school, she and Matthew will feel her absence deeply. She feels a sense of loss at the thought of a house without Anne's vitality and spirit in it. Matthew takes a more practical approach and assures Marilla that the railroad will bring Anne back to them often. To Matthew, Anne is still a little girl and he doesn't feel the threat of her growing up as Marilla does.

Enrichment

1. The theme of this chapter is Anne stepping from the world of childhood into the world of adulthood. The title of the chapter, "Where the Brook and River Meet," comes from a Longfellow poem called "Maidenhood" (located in the Appendix). Read this poem and write a paragraph explaining the symbolism of the chapter title. Is Anne reluctant to step into adulthood?

   This poem is about leaving the simplicity of childhood and stepping into adulthood with all of its pain and responsibility. Childhood is represented by the "brook" and adulthood by the "river." At the moment Anne is standing between them, on the brink of adulthood. Anne realizes the loss of the simplicity in her life and worries about the new responsibilities that come with adulthood. She plans to enjoy every last minute of her childhood and is somewhat reluctant to see it come to an end.

"Her head whirled and her heart beat until it hurt her."

Vocabulary

Write the meaning of each bold word or phrase.

1. with an air of **chastened*** triumph v. subdued; restrained
2. But she did hope **fervently** adv. with intense passion; ardently
3. I haven't got the **grit** to go there n. endurance, strength of character
4. **sibilant** and rustling from the stir of poplars. adj. characterized by a hissing sound
5. it seemed so vain and **presumptuous** adj. overbearingly confident, arrogant
6. murmured a prayer of gratitude and **aspiration** n. a strong desire to achieve an end; ambition

*Look up "chasten" in the dictionary, and write out the complete definition, the alternate forms, and 2-3 synonyms. v. 1. to punish or reprimand for the sake of improvement

2. to restrain or subdue

synonyms: humble, control, check, suppress, discipline, correct

Expressions for Discussion

1. *"It does seem as if it was the end of everything, doesn't it?"* - Diana

   What is ending for Anne and Diana? *their school days together at Avonlea school*
2. *"Oh, we have had jolly times, haven't we, Anne?"* - Diana
3. *"There are times and seasons even yet when I don't feel that I've made any great headway in learning to like Josie Pye!"* - Anne

   What has Josie done to offend Anne this time? *Josie told Anne she looked awful and that she didn't think she was strong enough to get through the teacher's course.*
4. *"Just one awful moment—Diana, I felt exactly as I did four years ago when I asked Marilla if I might stay at Green Gables—and then everything cleared up in my mind and my heart began beating again …"* - Anne

   What was that "awful moment" for Anne? *the moment the exams were to begin*
5. *"I'm just dazzled inside."* - Anne

   What has dazzled Anne? *seeing her name at the top of the pass list*
6. *"Well now, I always said it. I knew you could beat them all easy."* - Matthew
7. *"I just guess she has done well, and far be it from me to be backward in saying it."* - Mrs. Lynde

   Who is the one person who hides her pride in Anne's success? *Marilla*

Comprehension Questions

Answer the following in complete sentences.

1. What is Miss Stacy's advice to the students for occupying themselves the night before their tests?
   Miss Stacy advises her students not to open any books at all on the night before they take the tests. She says it will tire and confuse them and they would be better off with a walk and an early night.

2. How does Moody Spurgeon steady his nerves? Moody repeats the multiplication tables to himself to steady his nerves. He thinks it keeps all the facts in his head in their proper places.

3. What is Anne's "nobler motive" for wishing to do well on the Queen's test? Anne wishes to achieve honors on the Queen's test for the sake of Matthew and Marilla. Matthew's complete confidence in Anne's abilities inspires her to want to please him and see his eyes light up with pride in her.

4. What is Matthew's expectation of Anne's success on the test? Does she meet his expectation?
   Matthew declares that Anne will come in first on the test. She does meet his expectation as she ties with Gilbert for first place.

Enrichment

1. Mrs. Lynde's opinion is stated several times in this chapter. Add to your list of "Mrs. Lynde maxims."
   If you can't be cheerful, be as cheerful as you can; the sun will go on rising and setting whether Anne fails in geometry or not; the delay in the posting of the pass list is only to be expected with a Tory superintendent of education.

... she recited as she had never done before.

Reading Notes

organdy a stiff transparent fabric of cotton or silk
toilet the act or process of dressing or grooming oneself
brocade a heavy fabric interwoven with a rich, raised design
bumpkin an awkward, unsophisticated person

Vocabulary

Write the meaning of each bold word or phrase.

1. from which Anne was for ever **debarred**. v. excluded; shut out
2. a **gaunt** figure with greyer hair adj. thin and bony
3. look at our **elocutionist** n. a clear and expressive speaker
4. She was a **lithe**, dark-eyed woman adj. flexible, supple, slender
5. At this **unpropitious*** moment adj. unlucky; unfavorable
6. at once triumphant and **taunting**. adj. insulting; ridiculing

*Look up "propitious" and "unpropitious" in the dictionary, and write out the complete definition, the alternate forms, and 2-3 synonyms for both words.

propitious: adj. favorable, advantageous *alternate forms:* propitiously - adv. propitiousness - n.
synonyms: lucky, fortunate, happy, providential, suitable, auspicious, timely
unpropitious: adj. not propitious *alternate forms:* unpropitiously - adv. unpropitiousness - n.
synonyms: unfavorable, unlucky, untimely

Expressions for Discussion

1. *"I have given up all hope of dimples. My dimple-dream will never come true; but so many of my dreams have that I mustn't complain."* - Anne
2. *"There's something so stylish about you, Anne. You hold your head with such an air."* - Diana
3. *"Time was when he took my advice, but now he just buys things for Anne regardless ... Just let them tell him a thing is pretty and fashionable, and Matthew plunks his money down for it."* - Marilla
   What has Matthew bought for Anne? *purple organdy material for a dress*
4. *"It's new every morning, and I feel as if I washed my very soul in that bath of earliest sunshine."* - Anne
5. *"... I'd rather make people cry than laugh."* - Anne
   When would Anne rather make people cry than laugh? *when she is reciting, so she always chooses sad pieces to recite*

6. *"Who is that girl on the platform with the splendid Titian hair? She has a face I should like to paint."*
- a famous American painter Who is the girl with Titian hair? *Anne*

7. *"I'm quite content to be Anne of Green Gables, with my string of pearl beads."* - Anne
Where did Anne get her pearl beads? *from Matthew*

Comprehension Questions

Answer the following in complete sentences.

1. What is the "epoch" in Anne's life in this chapter? Why is it an epoch? Performing in the concert is an epoch in Anne's life because it is an honor to be chosen, and Anne dreamed of that honor years ago when she first attended a concert. It is a representation of Anne's maturity and reputation in the community.

2. What is Marilla's regret about the night of the concert? Marilla's regret is that she can't attend the concert and hear Anne's recitation.

3. Why does Anne decide she will "hate that white-lace girl to the end of life"? The white-lace girl makes fun of the audience in a derogatory way, referring to them as "country bumpkins" and "rustic belles." Anne resents this since these are the people she has grown up with and loves. She appreciates them as they are and can't tolerate them being belittled.

4. How does Anne recover from her stage fright? Anne sees Gilbert Blythe at the back of the room and thinks he is smiling triumphantly and tauntingly at Anne's stage fright. The determination not to fail in front of Gilbert gives her the courage to give the best performance she has ever given

5. When Jane is wishing for riches, Anne tells her they are already rich. In what ways does Anne say they are rich? They have sixteen years to their credit, they are happy as queens, and they all have imaginations. They have a future that stretches before them as a 'vision of things not seen.' And they have an appreciation of the nature around them that they couldn't enjoy more if they had millions of dollars and ropes of diamonds.

Enrichment

1. Read "The Maiden's Vow" (located in the Appendix) aloud several times. Then, see if you can give an Anne-worthy performance and make your audience cry.

Reading Notes

Providence the occurrence of events that have been divinely guided by a deity

duck slang for a peculiar person

Avery scholarship two hundred and fifty dollars a year for four years at Redmond College awarded to the person with the highest grade in English

B. A. a person holding a Bachelor of Arts degree

Vocabulary

Write the meaning of each bold word or phrase.

1. he walked **agitatedly** across the yard adv. in a disturbed or excited manner
2. **acutely** and miserably conscious adv. severely; intensely
3. as she reflected **pessimistically**. adv. negatively; hopelessly
4. Anne's highest **pinnacle** of aspiration n. summit, peak
5. a teacher's **provincial*** licence n. rural; limited
6. whether one would be **allotted** to Queen's v. given or distributed officially

*Look up "provincial" in the dictionary, and write out the complete definition, the alternate forms, and 2-3 synonyms. adj. & n. adj. 1. of or pertaining to a province 2. unsophisticated; uncultured; limited in outlook n. 1. an inhabitant of a province 2. an unsophisticated person
alternate forms: provinciality - n. provincialize - v. provincially - adv.
adj. syn.: rustic, uncultured, unpolished, unrefined *n. syn.:* rustic, yokel, country bumpkin

Expressions for Discussion

1. *"Now, I call that a positive triumph."* - Anne
   What is Anne's "positive triumph"? *Marilla crying over her recitation of "The Maiden's Vow"*
   What is the real reason Marilla was crying? *She was wishing Anne had stayed a little girl and not grown up.*
2. *"And I was wishing you could have stayed a little girl, even with all your queer ways."* - Marilla
3. *"I'm not a bit changed—not really. I'm only just pruned down and branched out."* - Anne
   What does it mean to be "pruned down and branched out"? *Anne is comparing her growth and maturity to that of a tree that flourishes after being pruned. Marilla and Matthew have "pruned" Anne so that she is now a mature young lady.*
4. *"I guess my putting in my oar occasional never did much harm after all."* - Matthew
5. *"What a splendid chin he has! I never noticed it before."* - Anne
   Whose chin is Anne admiring? *Gilbert's*
6. *"I won't cry. It's silly—and weak—there's the third tear splashing down by my nose."* - Anne
   Why is Anne crying? *because she is homesick*

7. *"I'll win that scholarship if hard work can do it."* - Anne

8. *"... That's the best of it. Just as soon as you attain to one ambition you see another one glittering higher up still. It does make life so interesting."* - Anne

   What ambition has Anne seen fulfilled recently? *passing the Queen's exams at the top of the list*
   What is Anne's new ambition? *to win the scholarship to Redmond College*

Comprehension Questions

Answer the following in complete sentences.

1. Who sees to it that Anne has plenty of clothes? Matthew sees to it that Anne has plenty of clothes.

2. How does Matthew credit Providence with the mistake that resulted in Anne coming to live at Green Gables? *Matthew thinks it was Providence that brought Anne into their lives because God saw that they needed her.

3. How does Marilla react to Anne's departure from Avonlea? Marilla makes herself busy with needless work as she tries to deal with a heartache that burns and gnaws at her. Then she goes to Anne's gable room, buries her face in the pillow, and weeps in a passion of sobs.

4. How does Anne feel about sharing the classroom at Queen's with Gilbert? Anne is comforted that Gilbert is in her class. She is excited that their old rivalry can continue on. She also notices his splendid chin.

5. How does Josie Pye manage to insult Anne when she comes to visit? Josie tells Anne that she shouldn't cry because it makes her nose and eyes get red and then she seems red all over. She also tells Anne that she informed a boy in class that Anne was an orphan and nobody knew much about what she'd been before the Cuthberts adopted her.

6. What would winning the Avery scholarship provide for Anne? For whom does she want to win the scholarship? The Avery scholarship provides for a four-year college course that would give Anne a degree much higher than a teaching certificate. She wants to win it for herself because she is ambitious, but she really wants to win it for the sake of Matthew.

Enrichment

1. Write a paragraph contrasting luck and Providence. What is the difference? Do you think luck or Providence figure more actively in Anne's life?

   Luck is the random occurrence of events as chance happenings, uninfluenced by a deity.
   Providence is the occurrence of events that have been divinely guided by a deity.

Reading Notes

Stella Maynard one of Anne's new friends at the Academy; "rose-red" with black eyes; has a heartful of wistful dreams and fancies

Priscilla Grant one of Anne's new friends at the Academy; "dream girl"; pale and spiritual-looking; full of mischief and pranks and fun

Frank Stockley a boy at the Academy; has more "dash and go," but not half as good-looking as Gilbert

Vocabulary

Write the meaning of each bold word or phrase.

1. all the Queen's scholars had **gravitated** v. moved or attracted to some source
2. the most stylish **modes** of hair-dressing n. ways of doing things; methods; techniques
3. attained a certain **pre-eminence** n. supremacy; that which surpasses all others
4. life would be **insupportable** adj. intolerable; unjustifiable
5. you could not regard them **philosophically**. adv. in a wise and calm manner
6. to be woven into an immortal **chaplet**. n. a garland for the head

Expressions for Discussion

1. *"That Anne-girl improves all the time."* - Miss Barry

2. *"Girls, sometimes I feel as if those exams meant everything, but when I look at the big buds swelling on those chestnut trees and the misty blue air at the end of the streets they don't seem half so important."* - Anne

3. *"That may make me feel badly tomorrow, Josie …"* - Anne

   What has Josie said to make Anne feel badly? *She said that a professor has predicted the winners of the scholarship and medal, and Anne is not one of them.*

4. *"I've done my best, and I begin to understand what is meant by the 'joy of the strife.'"* - Anne

   Define "strife" in this context. How can there be joy in strife? *Strife is a struggle or conflict. The joy of strife would be overcoming a difficult situation. Anne has the satisfaction of knowing she did the best she could, so even if she fails, her victory is in her commitment and hard work. A perfect example of this is the Apostle Paul's summary of his Christian walk in 2 Timothy 4:7 (I have fought a good fight, I have finished my course, I have kept the faith).*

Comprehension Questions

Answer the following in complete sentences.

1. What is Anne's attitude about boys? How is she feeling about Gilbert at this time? Anne feels that boys would make good comrades and furnish broader standpoints of judgment and comparison. In other words, it would be nice to have the companionship of boys to get their viewpoints, which would naturally be different from the viewpoints of her girlfriends. Anne is becoming interested in boys and curious about them, but her interest is not fully developed in the sense that she is ready to think of them as lovers.

2. How has Anne's attitude toward competition with Gilbert changed? Anne's rivalry with Gilbert is still as intense as it has ever been, but it doesn't have the bitterness in it anymore that characterized it previously. Rather than being motivated by winning in order to defeat Gilbert, Anne is now motivated by winning a victory over a worthy foeman. She now sees Gilbert as a rival worthy of respect, and a victory over him represents a job well completed, not the downfall of her rival.

3. Anne says that the next best thing to "trying and winning" is "trying and failing." What does this statement mean? Anne realizes that there is value in trying, even if one doesn't succeed. Making an attempt to accomplish a goal is much better than never even trying because of the fear of failure. One can be proud of one's effort, even if the effort doesn't result in victory. The real victory is in the perseverance and commitment to a task.

4. What is Anne doing while the other girls are talking about what they are going to wear to commencement? Anne gazes out the window and daydreams about her future and the possibilities before her as the other girls talk about trivial matters.

Enrichment

1. Anne has an appreciation of the beauty of nature that sees her through dark times in her life. Find a place that represents the beauty of nature to you, and draw a picture of it.

Vocabulary

Write the meaning of each bold word or phrase.

1. **amid** hearty cheers. prep. among; in the midst of
2. her hands shaken **vigorously**. adv. energetically
3. **Commencement** was the next important happening. n. graduation
4. Josie said you were **infatuated*** with her. adj. bewitched; captivated
5. I think he has only been its **nominal** head adj. in name only
6. that cold, **sanctifying** touch adj. purifying; holy

*Look up "infatuated" in the dictionary, and write out the complete definition, the alternate forms, and 2-3 synonyms. adj. affected by foolish or unreasoning fondness

synonyms: obsessed, fascinated, enchanted, beguiled, besotted, enamored, captivated

Expressions for Discussion

1. *"And I'm not going to march up to that bulletin board and look at it before everybody. I haven't the moral courage."* - Anne
   What is on the bulletin board? *the announcement of the winners of the scholarship and medal*
2. *"Reckon you're glad we kept her, Marilla?"* - Matthew
   What is Marilla's reply? *(Expression #3 below)*
3. *"It's not the first time I've been glad. You do like to rub things in, Matthew Cuthbert."* - Marilla
4. *"But just now I feel as if it were joy enough to sit here and look at you."* - Anne
   Who is Anne content to look at? *Diana*
5. *"Well now, I'd rather have you than a dozen boys, Anne. Just mind you that—rather than a dozen boys."* - Matthew
   Where are Anne and Matthew? *walking together as they lead the cows into the pasture for the night*

Comprehension Questions

Answer the following in complete sentences.

1. The author says, "We pay a price for everything we get or take in this world." What is the price we pay for ambition? Ambition exacts the price of hard work, self-denial in a commitment to that work, and the anxiety and discouragement that come with the uncertainty of success.

2. Who wins the Queen's medal? Who wins the Avery scholarship? Gilbert Blythe wins the Queen's medal and Anne wins the Avery scholarship.

3. What is the first thing Anne says upon learning of her victory? Upon learning of her victory, Anne says, "Oh, won't Matthew and Marilla be pleased!"

4. What is Mrs. Lynde's opinion about higher education for women? Mrs. Lynde does not believe in the higher education of women because she says it makes them unfit for "woman's true sphere." She would be of the attitude that once a woman has received a higher education, she will no longer be satisfied with her role as housekeeper, wife, and mother; she will begin wishing for things that should only belong in the world of men.

5. How does Anne spend "the last night before sorrow touched her life"? Anne spends the evening in companionship with Matthew as he brings the cows in for the night. Matthew tells Anne that he would rather have her than a dozen boys and that he is proud of her.

Enrichment

1. Anne says, "And that tea-rose—why, it's a song and a hope and a prayer all in one." How can a rose be a song, a hope, and a prayer?

   Anne's appreciation of the things of nature leads her to see all kinds of promise in one simple rose. The rose is a song in the way that music uplifts us and inspires us. It is a hope because it represents life and the joy that comes with life. It is a prayer of thanksgiving and acknowledgement of a God who created beauty and is in control of all things.

For the first time shy, quiet Matthew Cuthbert was a person of central importance.

Reading Notes

Abbey Bank the bank that held all the Cuthberts' savings and went bankrupt

Martin the Cuthberts' hired man

John Blythe Gilbert's father; Marilla's old beau

Vocabulary

Write the meaning of each bold word or phrase.

1. she turned sick and **pallid**. adj. pale; sickly
2. the old house was hushed and **tranquil***. adj. serene; peaceful
3. framing his **placid** face adj. calm, peaceful
4. Marilla's **impassioned** grief adj. deeply felt; passionate
5. her first **vigil** with sorrow. n. watch; observation
6. in its smooth inner **convolutions**. n. windings; curves

*Look up "tranquil" in the dictionary, and write out the complete definition, the alternate forms, and 2-3 synonyms. adj. calm, without motion or sound; free from emotional or mental disturbance

alternate forms: tranquility - n. tranquilly - adv.

synonyms: quiet, peaceful, placid, still, self-controlled, composed

Expressions for Discussion

1. *"When you've seen that look as often as I have you'll know what it means."* - Mrs. Lynde
   Who is she looking at? *Matthew, directly after his collapse*
2. *"I want to be quite silent and quiet and try to realize it. I can't realize it."* - Anne
   To whom is Anne speaking? *Diana*
3. *"… She's good and kind and sweet—but it's not her sorrow—she's outside of it and she couldn't come close enough to my heart to help me. It's our sorrow—yours and mine."* - Anne
   Who is outside of Anne's sorrow? *Diana*
   Who is close enough to Anne's heart to help her? *Marilla*
4. *"… You mustn't think I didn't love you as well as Matthew did, for all that. … I love you as dear as if you were my own flesh and blood and you've been my joy and comfort ever since you came to Green Gables."* - Marilla
   Why do you think Marilla finally opens up and tells Anne how she feels about her? *Death makes mortality real and makes people realize the need to express their feelings to others before it is too late.*
5. *"I did use to think you were possessed."* - Marilla
   Who did Marilla think was possessed? *Anne*
   Why? *Anne was constantly getting into scrapes that Marilla had to extricate her from.*
6. *"Marilla, I've almost decided to give up trying to like Josie Pye. I've made what I would once have called a heroic effort to like her, but Josie Pye won't be liked."* - Anne
   What has Josie said to Anne now? *Josie said that Anne's hair is redder than ever and she wondered if people who had red hair ever got used to it.*

Comprehension Questions

Answer the following in complete sentences.

1. What is the shock that precipitates Matthew's death? The shock that precipitates Matthew's death is the announcement of the closure of the bank in which his life savings was deposited. It represents financial failure for Matthew and Marilla.

2. What is the thought that finally releases Anne's tears? The thought that finally releases Anne's tears is the memory of Matthew the night before telling her, "My girl—my girl that I'm proud of."

3. Why can Anne share her grief with Marilla, but not with Diana? Diana loves Anne, but she is outside of Anne's sorrow because she didn't love Matthew like Anne did. She can sympathize with Anne, but she can't empathize. Anne's sorrow is outside of Diana's sphere of experience. Anne's sorrow belongs to her and Marilla alone because they are Matthew's family and share the same feelings about him.

4. When Anne feels guilty for beginning to take joy in life again, how does Mrs. Allan comfort her? *Mrs. Allan tells Anne that Matthew liked to hear her laugh and to know that she took pleasure in the world around her. Even though he is no longer on earth, Matthew would still want to know that Anne had not lost her joy in life and would want her to move beyond her grief and begin living fully again.

5. Who does Anne wish is in heaven to meet Matthew when he arrives? Anne wishes the souls of all the little white roses that Matthew loved every summer are in heaven to greet him.

6. What is Marilla's secret romance? Gilbert Blythe's father was Marilla's beau when she was young. They had an argument and she refused to forgive him when he asked her to. When Marilla was finally ready to forgive him, he never came back, so she lost her chance.

Enrichment

1. Copy the dialogue between Anne and Marilla as they share their grief in the middle of the night. Have you ever experienced a sorrow that you felt you couldn't share with people who were outside of it? If so, tell about it in a paragraph.

Reading Notes

oculist a former term for an ophthalmologist; eye doctor
John Sadler man from Carmody; wants to buy Green Gables

Vocabulary

Write the meaning of each bold word or phrase.

1. Something in her **dejected** attitude adj. downcast; discouraged
2. Marilla sit limply **inert*** like that. adj. unable to move or act; sluggish
3. in defiance of the oculist's **prohibition** n. forbiddance; restriction
4. a glory of soft mingled **hues** n. shades; colors
5. said Gilbert, **jubilantly**. adv. joyfully
6. and **congenial** friendship adj. pleasant because of having similar interests

*Look up "inert" in the dictionary, and write out the complete definition, the alternate forms, and 2-3 synonyms. adj. unable to move or act; sluggish
alternate forms: inertly - adv. inertness - n.
synonyms: motionless, immobile, static, stationary, slow

Expressions for Discussion

1. *"You surely don't think I could leave you alone in your trouble, Marilla, after all you've done for me."* - Anne
2. *"Nothing could be worse than giving up Green Gables—nothing could hurt me more."* - Anne
3. *"I shall give life here my best, and I believe it will give its best to me in return."* - Anne
4. *"But I can't let you sacrifice yourself so for me. It would be terrible."* - Marilla
   What is Anne giving up for Marilla? *her scholarship to Redmond*
5. *"Oh, Marilla, don't you go pitying me. I don't like to be pitied, and there is no need for it. I'm heart glad over the very thought of staying at dear Green Gables."* - Anne
6. *"I feel as if you'd give me new life."* - Marilla
7. *"There's a good deal of the child about her yet in some ways."* - Mrs. Lynde
8. *"Dear old world, you are very lovely, and I am glad to be alive in you."* - Anne

Comprehension Questions

Answer the following in complete sentences.

1. Why is Marilla being forced to sell Green Gables? Marilla's eyesight is deteriorating and she is threatened with blindness. She doesn't feel she can run the farm by herself, even with the help of a hired man. She has no savings since the bank collapse, and money is owed on the farm. So Marilla doesn't have a choice but to sell the farm so that she has some money to live on.

2. What is Anne's plan to save Green Gables? Anne determines to give up the Avery scholarship and teach locally so that she can live with Marilla and help her. She has made plans for Mr. Barry to rent the farm so that she and Marilla will have an income.

3. What does Gilbert do for Anne? How does this affect their relationship? Gilbert gives up his teaching job at Avonlea so that Anne can have it and live at home with Marilla. Gilbert is going to teach at White Sands and work to earn his way through college, so he has sacrificed for Anne because now he is going to have to pay for his boarding as well as his education. Anne is very appreciative to Gilbert for his sacrifice and tells him that her pride and stubbornness prevented her from admitting that she forgave him the day he rescued her. They agree to be good friends and to help each other in the future.

4. Explain the meaning of the chapter title. What is Anne's "bend in the road"? Anne had her future laid out smoothly when Matthew died and everything changed. Anne's "bend in the road" is the death of Matthew that forces her to change her plans and take a different path in her life. It is no longer a straight road that she can see clearly, but Anne embraces it with the commitment to duty and love for the people in her life that we have come to expect from her.

Enrichment

1. The author says of Anne, "She had looked her duty courageously in the face and found it a friend—as duty ever is when we meet it frankly." How can one's duty be one's friend?
   The satisfaction one receives from doing one's duty can far outweigh the disappointment in having to give something up to do one's duty. Putting others before oneself results in a clear conscience and the assurance that one is acting in a Christ-like manner. In that way, duty becomes one's friend.

2. Anne has an inner peace that rises above all difficulties. Where do you think Anne's strength of mind comes from? Write a composition exploring this theme, using examples from the story of Anne's life that you have just read.
   Possible answers include: Anne's strength of mind comes from being brought up by Matthew and Marilla; Anne's difficult early life which gives her an inner strength to survive; Anne's imagination which allows her to relate to and empathize with others; Anne's intelligence which provides her with the tools to recognize the important things in life; Anne's faith which has been cultivated with Marilla's influence.

Expressions for Discussion

1. *"I can't tell you the person's name because I have vowed never to let it cross my lips."*
   a. Who said it? Anne
   b. Whose name will never cross Anne's lips? Gilbert's
2. *"What would you feel like if a white thing did snatch me up and carry me off?"*
   a. Who said it? Anne
   b. What was the response? "I'll risk it."
3. *"Oh, no, it takes me to make such a mistake."*
   a. What is Anne's mistake this time? flavoring a cake with anodyne liniment
4. *"I really don't see how I'm going to live through the two weeks before school begins, I'm so impatient to see her."*
   a. Who is Anne impatient to see? the new Avonlea school teacher
5. *"… The thought that it is all my own fault is what makes it so hard. If I could blame it on anybody I would feel so much better."*
   a. What is Anne's fault? breaking her ankle
6. *"If I had been killed she would have had to carry a dark burden of remorse all her life."*
   a. Who was almost killed? Anne
   b. Who would have had to carry a dark burden of remorse? Josie Pye
7. *"When she pronounces my name I feel instinctively that she's spelling it with an* e*."*
   a. Who does Anne feel instinctively spells her name correctly? Miss Stacy
8. *"Don't be alarmed if you hear me groaning."*
   a. Who is groaning? Anne
   b. Why is she groaning? She has to groan in a recitation she is doing.
9. *"I knew he was up to some foolishness."*
   a. Who said it? Marilla
   b. Who is up to foolishness? Matthew
   c. What is that foolishness? getting a dress with puffed sleeves made for Anne
10. *"It did seem to me that I'd never get over it if they went out before I had a dress with them. I'd never have felt quite satisfied, you see."*
    a. What is it that Anne wanted before it went out of style? a dress with puffed sleeves
11. *"We're going to keep them all sacredly and have them to read to our descendants."*
    a. What are Anne and her friends going to have to read to their descendants? their stories
12. *"Anne's a great hand at explaining."*
    a. Who said it? Matthew
    b. What does Anne need to explain? why she doesn't have tea ready

13. *"Little things like that are of no important now because I don't suppose I'll ever be able to go anywhere again. My career is closed."*

  a. Who said it? Anne

  b. Why is her career closed? She dyed her hair and it turned green.

14. *"You don't think much about romance when you have just escaped from a watery grave."*

  a. What is the watery grave Anne has just escaped from? drowning as the Lady of Shalott

15. *"If I'd a child like Anne in the house all the time I'd be a better and happier woman."*

  a. Who said it? Miss Josephine Barry

16. *"… he takes them spells oftener than he used to and I'm anxious about him."*

  a. Who said it? Marilla

  b. Who is taking spells? Matthew

17. *"I did make a mistake in judging Anne, but it weren't no wonder, for an odder, unexpecteder witch of a child there never was in this world, that's what."*

  a. Who said it? Mrs. Rachel Lynde

18. *"Oh, you good old friends, I'm glad to see your honest face once more …"*

  a. Who are Anne's good old friends? her school books

19. *"It does seem as if it was the end of everything, doesn't it?"*

  a. Who said it? Diana

  b. What is ending? their school years together

20. *"I'm just dazzled inside."*

  a. What has dazzled Anne? winning first place on the Queen's test

21. *"I'd rather make people cry than laugh."*

  a. When would Anne rather make people cry? when she is reciting

22. *"Now, I call that a positive triumph."*

  a. What is Anne's triumph? Marilla crying at her recitation

23. *"What a splendid chin he has! I never noticed it before."*

  a. Who has a splendid chin? Gilbert

24. *"That Anne-girl improves all the time."*

  a. Who said it? Miss Josephine Barry

25. *"It's not the first time I've been glad. You do like to rub things in, Matthew Cuthbert."*

  a. Who said it? Marilla

  b. What is she glad about? that they adopted Anne

26. *"Well, now, I'd rather have you than a dozen boys, Anne. Just mind you that—rather than a dozen boys."*

  a. Who said it? Matthew

27. *"When you've seen that look as often as I have you'll know what it means."*

   a. Who said it? Mrs. Lynde

   b. What is she looking at? Matthew's face after he's collapsed

28. *"… She's good and kind and sweet—but it's not her sorrow—she's outside of it and she couldn't come close enough to my heart to help me. It's our sorrow—yours and mine."*

   a. Who is outside of Anne's sorrow? Diana

   b. Who is close enough to Anne's heart to help her? Marilla

29. *"I did use to think you were possessed."*

   a. Who said it? Marilla

30. *"Nothing could be worse than giving up Green Gables—nothing could hurt me more."*

   a. Who said it? Anne

31. *"But I can't let you sacrifice yourself so for me. It would be terrible."*

   a. Who said it? Marilla

   b. What is the sacrifice being made? Anne is giving up her scholarship to college.

32. *"I feel as if you'd give me new life."*

   a. Who said it? Marilla

Who Am I?

1. Anne's beloved minister's wife Mrs. Allan
2. Anne's favorite minister Mr. Allan
3. the Sunday School Superintendent Mr. Bell
4. Anne's friend who always insults her Josie Pye
5. Anne's inspiring teacher Miss Stacy
6. Anne's friend who is going to be a minister Moody Spurgeon

Short Answer

1. What mistake does Anne make when Mrs. Allan comes to tea?
   She accidentally flavors a cake with anodyne liniment.
2. What does Anne think would turn her into a model child? being invited to tea every day
3. Why could Anne never be a minister's wife? She will never be naturally good.
4. How does Anne hurt herself when she falls from the ridge-pole? She breaks her ankle.
5. What does Marilla realize when Anne is injured? Anne is dear to her.
6. What wish does Anne have granted when she is injured? She faints.

7. What is Marilla's attitude about Miss Stacy's Christmas concert? She thinks it is a bunch of nonsense and will waste the students' time.

8. What does Matthew give Anne for Christmas? a dress with puffed sleeves

9. What does Aunt Josephine give Anne for Christmas? a pair of kid slippers

10. Which does Anne think is the more romantic ending to a story, a funeral or a wedding? a funeral

11. What is Anne's "besetting sin"? daydreaming

12. How does Diana solve the problem of ending her stories? She kills everyone.

13. Why was Anne willing to be a "little wicked" by dyeing her hair? It was worth a little wickedness to get rid of red hair.

14. What role does Anne play when the girls reenact "Lancelot and Elaine"? Elaine

15. Who rescues Anne from a "watery grave"? Gilbert

16. What does Anne say is the best part of her trip to the city to visit Aunt Josephine? coming home

17. What is Anne's regret when Gilbert seeks peace and friendship between them? She rejects his offer.

18. How does Moody Spurgeon steady his nerves? by reciting the multiplication tables

19. Who is convinced that Anne will excel on the Queen's test before she ever takes it? Matthew

20. Who gives Anne a string of pearl beads? Matthew

21. How does Anne recover from stage fright? She refuses to fail in front of Gilbert.

22. Who wins the Queen's medal? Gilbert the Avery scholarship? Anne

23. What is the shock that precipitates Matthew's death? the failing of the bank

24. How does Anne save Green Gables? She gives up her college scholarship to stay home and teach.

25. What does Gilbert do for Anne to make her sacrifice easier? He gives up teaching at the Avonlea school so she can teach there.

26. How has Mrs. Lynde's opinion of Anne changed by the end of the book? She admits she made a mistake in her original judgment of Anne, and that Marilla and Matthew were right to adopt her.

27. How does Anne's opinion of Gilbert change by the end of the book? Anne finally forgives Gilbert and accepts his friendship and help.

28. What is Anne's "bend in the road"? the death of Matthew

Comprehension Questions

1. Describe Anne's relationship with Matthew. How does it differ from her relationship with Marilla? Matthew falls in love with Anne almost immediately. He is delighted with her conversation and appreciation for the world. He is fully confident that she will excel in whatever she attempts and lavishes praise on her when she does succeed. He is a ready listener and always gives her the benefit of the doubt. He is openly affectionate and loving to Anne. Marilla doesn't often tell Anne how much she loves her. And since Marilla has the responsibility of raising Anne, it falls on her to be the rule-maker and disciplinarian.

2. How does Matthew credit Providence with the mistake that resulted in Anne coming to live at Green Gables? Matthew originally decides that he and Marilla should adopt Anne because she needs them. But, ultimately, he comes to the conclusion that God brought Anne to them because they needed her in their lives. He is thankful for God blessing them with Anne's presence.

3. When Anne feels guilty for beginning to take joy in life again after Matthew's death, how does Mrs. Allan comfort her? Mrs. Allan tells Anne that Matthew liked to hear her laugh and to know that she took pleasure in the world around her. Even though he is no longer on earth, Matthew would still want to know that Anne had not lost her joy in life and would want her to move beyond her grief and begin living fully again.

Mastery Word List

chasten	**eclipse**	**evince**	**implicit**
inert	**infatuated**	**inscrutable**	**pithy**
precarious	**propitious (un-)**	**prosaic**	**provincial**
quaint	**succumb**	**veracity/veracious**	

Synonym Substitution

Write a few good synonyms or a phrase in the blank to replace the highlighted word.

1. Due to his hard work over the summer, Anthony was able to **eclipse** all his records from the previous year. surpass, top, outshine
2. When dinner was over, she stacked all the plates **precariously** and attempted to take them to the kitchen without breaking them. unsteadily, shakily, in an insecure manner
3. Although the speaker was eloquent, he was in no way **pithy**. short, meaningful
4. "Never **succumb** to the temptation of bitterness." - Martin Luther King, Jr. give in to
5. The children were immediately **infatuated** when they saw the puppy behind the glass. enchanted, obsessed, enamored
6. Cats are usually **inert** during the day and active during the night. inactive, unable to move
7. His life in New York was quite different from the **provincial** experience of his hometown. uncultured, unsophisticated, naive
8. The only way to get out of this is to **evince** your innocence. demonstrate, prove
9. Marriage can only work if there is **implicit** trust. unwavering, unconditional
10. The **propitious** turn of events led to his being crowned king. lucky, fortunate, beneficial
11. Books can help us escape the **prosaic** and engage the whimsical. dull, boring, unimaginative
12. Mary was put off by her mother's **inscrutable** look. mysterious, hard to figure out
13. A smart child will soon learn to **chasten** his tongue. control, tame, restrain
14. It is not your passion that I doubt, but your **veracity**. truthfulness, honesty
15. The **quaint** town attracted all sorts of interesting people. unusual, odd

Mastery Substitution

Use a word from the Mastery Word List to replace the highlighted word or phrase.
You may have to change the form of the word to fit the sentence.

1. They sat there **unable to move** for the entire time she yelled at them. inert
2. Do not **fall victim** to fear. succumb
3. "A man is never more **truthful** than when he acknowledges himself a liar." - Mark Twain veracious
4. Much of the wisdom of a culture is displayed in **short but meaningful** phrases called proverbs. pithy
5. They couldn't break Ben of his **strange** habit of rearranging garden gnomes. quaint
6. "An unexciting truth may be **overshadowed** by a thrilling lie." - Aldous Huxley eclipsed
7. The poor travelers experienced one **unfortunate** event after another. unpropitious
8. The **local** governor tried to move beyond the **unsophisticated** ideas of his predecessor. provincial
9. You must **discipline** your heart and mind to prevent them from running wild. chasten
10. The sailor spoke **mysteriously** of some great monster out at sea. inscrutably
11. We were all sad to have to listen to his **unimaginative** retelling of the story. prosaic
12. His love for the team was **demonstrated** by the paraphernalia plastered all over his walls. evinced
13. The game of darts can become rather **perilous** when you blindfold the players. precarious
14. Bilbo grew more and more **obsessed** with the ring the longer he had it. infatuated
15. Summer brings with it the **understood** need for ice cream. implicit

Implementation

Use at least eight of the words from the Mastery Word List in a paragraph of your own.

Appendix

A
abasement .... humiliation; degradation
abashed .... embarrassed, disconcerted
abstracted .... preoccupied; lost in thought
actuated .... caused to move
acutely .... severely; intensely
admonished .... reprimanded, warned
aesthetic .... having to do with beauty
agitatedly .... in a disturbed or excited manner
albeit .... although
allayed .... relieved; alleviated
allotted .... given or distributed officially
amid .... among; in the midst of
arduous .... hard to achieve; difficult
askance .... with a sideways glance of disapproval
aspiration .... a strong desire to achieve an end
B
beatification .... making or being blessed
beaux .... (pl. of beau) admirers, boyfriends
bedizened .... adorned gaudily
beguiled .... distracted; charmed; entranced
behooved .... required; compelled
benevolent .... eager to do good; charitable
bent .... determined
bequeathed ... left to a person by will; handed down
beseechingly .... pleadingly; imploringly
bevy .... group
blazoned .... announced; proclaimed
blight .... a harmful or destructive force
blithely .... light-heartedly; carefreely
brusquely .... abruptly; bluntly
C
canto .... a division of a long poem
capricious .... unpredictable; fickle
chaplet .... a garland for the head
chastened .... subdued; restrained
cloistered .... sheltered; secluded
cogitation .... consideration; serious thought
commencement .... graduation
complacent .... self-satisfied; smug
compunction .... guilty conscience
confounded .... confused
congenial .... pleasant
consequent .... logically consistent
consolation .... comfort in time of grief
consternation .... anxiety causing confusion
contortions .... twistings; things in a twisted state
convolutions .... windings; curves
corroborated .... confirmed; supported
coruscations .... flashes; sparkles
countenance .... to support; to approve
cultivated .... intentionally improved or developed
curtly .... noticeably or rudely brief
D
debarred .... excluded; shut out
decorum .... polite behavior
deferring .... postponing
deftly .... skillfully
dejected .... downcast; discouraged
demure .... quiet; shy; reserved
deportment .... manners; behavior
deprecatingly .... with disapproval
dictum .... a formal saying; maxim
diligently .... showing care and effort
discerning .... showing good judgment or insight
discomfiture .... disappointment; frustration
disconsolately .... in an unhappy manner
discourse .... to converse; to talk
dissipation .... frivolous living
dolefully .... with mourning or sadness
drollery .... comedy; clowning
drudgery .... tiresome, unpleasant work
dubious .... uncertain, unreliable
dudgeon .... a feeling of great resentment; rage
dyspeptic .... subject to indigestion
E
eclipsed .... deprived of prominence; surpassed
effusion .... an outpouring, unrestrained flow
elocutionist .... a clear and expressive speaker
entreated .... pleaded; begged
epoch .... noteworthy, memorable event
estranged .... alienated; separated
ethereal .... airy, delicate, heavenly
evinced .... made evident, displayed
F
faltered .... stammered, stumbled
ferreted .... uncovered; hunted out
fervently .... with intense passion; ardently
fray .... a noisy fight or brawl
furbelows .... ruffles or frills on a skirt or petticoat
G
garret .... attic
gaunt .... thin and bony
gauntlet .... attack from all sides
gird .... to prepare for action
glens .... narrow, secluded valleys
glibly .... in a smooth but insincere manner
gravitated .... moved or attracted to some source
grit .... endurance, strength of character
H
hampered .... prevented or hindered
harrowing .... extremely distressing
haughtily ..... in an arrogantly self-admiring manner
heathen .... unbeliever; infidel
heedless .... thoughtless; unmindful
hues .... shades; colors
I
impassioned .... deeply felt; passionate
implicitly .... unquestioningly; without doubt
imploring .... begging earnestly, entreating
imposing .... impressive in appearance, formidable
inclination .... leaning; partiality
inculcate .... to persistently urge an idea or fact
inert .... unable to move; slow
inexorable .... unable to be persuaded, relentless
infatuated .... bewitched; captivated
inflection .... a change in the pitch of the voice
ingratiatingly .... in a pleasing or flattering manner
innovation .... new idea or method
inscrutable .... mysterious; incomprehensible
instinctively .... intuitively
insupportable .... intolerable; unjustifiable
intercepted .... interrupted; stopped
inveigled .... persuaded with cunning, enticed
irradiated .... shone upon; lit up
irreverence .... lack of reverence or due respect

J
jubilantly....................joyfully
K
kindred .... similar in nature
L
laudable .... praiseworthy; commendable
limpid....................clear; transparent
lithe....................flexible, supple, slender
ludicrously .... in an absurd or ridiculous manner
M
manse ....residence of a minister
martyr ....one who suffers or dies for a belief
modes... ways of doing things; methods; techniques
N
nom de plume.................... pen name; pseudonym
nominal....................in name only
O
obdurate ....stubborn; obstinate
obtrusive....................unpleasantly noticeable
officious .... meddlesome
opined ....held or expressed as an opinion
ostentatiously.............. in a showy, boastful manner
P
pallid .... pale; sickly
parsed....................dissected; broken down
penitent.................... a remorseful, repentant person
perquisites ....extra benefits, customary privileges
persistency....................perseverance; stubbornness
personified .... embodied in human form
perturbation .... a cause of disturbance or agitation
perusal ....careful reading
pervade ....to spread throughout; to permeate
pessimistically ....negatively; hopelessly
petition....................a request
philosophically .... in a wise and calm manner
pinions ....wings
pinnacle ....summit, peak
pithy .... short and forceful
placid.................... calm, peaceful
precarious....................unstable; insecure
precedence..... priority in time, order, or importance
predilection ....a preference or special liking
pre-eminence .... supremacy
prepense .... intentional, premeditated; planned
presentiment ....a vague expectation; omen
presumptuous..... overbearingly confident, arrogant
prima donna........ .leading female soloist in an opera
prohibition.................... forbiddance; restriction
prosaic....................unromantic, dull
providential..............marked by divine intervention
provincial.................... rural; limited
Q
quaint .... unusual, odd
qualms .... uneasy sense of doubt; concerns
R
rapt ....delighted; deeply moved
rebukingly .... reproachfully; disapprovingly
recourse .... a source of help; refuge
refractory .... stubborn, rebellious
refrain....................to avoid doing; to abstain
reiterated .... repeated
relented .... yielded to compassion, shown mercy
rendered ....made
reprehensible .... objectionable; unacceptable
reproachfully .... disapprovingly, rebukingly
resolute .... determined; decided
retaliatory .... punishing; vengeful
revelled ....delighted
reverie ....daydream
rigmarole ....a rambling or meaningless story
ruddy ....rosy; healthy
rue....................to regret
S
sagely .... wisely
sallow ....a sickly yellow
sanctifying .... purifying; holy
sated .... satisfied; gratified
sceptically....... in a questioning manner; doubtingly
scope....................range, extent of room
scrutinizingly..... with close examination; piercingly
sear .... scorched or withered
seraph.................... angel
sibilant...................characterized by a hissing sound
sojourn ....visit; stopover
sonorous .... having a full, rich sound
spasmodic....................convulsive; given to fits
sprite .... elf or fairy
staunchly .... faithfully, loyally
stipulations....................requirements; demands
subjective .... personal; nonobjective
sublime ....supreme; splendid
succession ....one after another
succumbed ....yielded; surrendered
superfluous .... more than enough, excess
supplicant....................humble beggar
suppositions .... assumptions; ideas
T
tableau......... a frozen scene (usually from history or literature)
tacitly................in a manner that is implied, silently
tartly ....sharply; bitterly
taunting ....insulting; ridiculing
tempestuous....................wild; unruly
tenacity........... unwillingness to let go, stubbornness
torrent ....outpouring; flow
tranquil .... serene; peaceful
tremulous .... timid; fearful
tribulations .... trials; sufferings
U
undauntedly.................... without fear; courageously
unheeded.................... disregarded, unnoticed
unpropitious ....unlucky; unfavorable
unregenerate .... sinful; obstinately bad
unwarranted .... groundless; unjustified
V
vagaries....................strange ideas or acts
vale .... valley
veracity .... truthfulness; honesty
verging.................... bordering
vexed ....angered; irritated
vigil.................... watch; observation
vigorously .... energetically
vim....................strength; energy
vivacity .... liveliness, animation
W
wonted .... usual; customary

From *Romeo and Juliet*

William Shakespeare
Act II, Scene ii, lines 38-48:

Juliet: 'Tis but thy name that is my enemy.
Thou art thyself, though not a Montague,
What's Montague? It is nor hand, nor foot,
Nor arm, nor face, nor any other part
Belonging to a man. Oh, be some other name!
What's in a name? That which we call a rose
By any other name would smell as sweet.
So Romeo would, were he not Romeo called,
Retain that dear perfection which he owes
Without that title. Romeo, doff thy name,
And for thy name, which is no part of thee,
Take all myself.

The Race that Long in Darkness Pined

John Morrison
Scottish Paraphrases, 1781

The race that long in darkness pined,
Have seen a glorious Light;
The people dwell in day, who dwelt
In death's surrounding night.
To hail Thy rise, Thou better Sun,
The gathering nations come,
Joyous as when the reapers bear
The harvest treasures home.
For Thou our burden hast removed,
And quelled the oppressor's sway,
Quick as the slaughtered squadrons fell
In Midian's evil day.
To us a Child of Hope is born,
To us a Son is given,
Him shall the tribes of earth obey,
Him all the hosts of heaven.
His Name shall be the Prince of Peace,
Forevermore adored,
The Wonderful, the Counselor,
The great and mighty Lord.
His power increasing still shall spread,
His reign no end shall know:
Justice shall guard His throne above,
And peace abound below.

Evelyn Hope

Robert Browning

I.
Beautiful Evelyn Hope is dead!
Sit and watch by her side an hour.
That is her book-shelf, this her bed;
She plucked that piece of geranium-flower,
Beginning to die too, in the glass;
Little has yet been changed, I think:
The shutters are shut, no light may pass
Save two long rays thro' the hinge's chink.

II.
Sixteen years old when she died!
Perhaps she had scarcely heard my name;
It was not her time to love; beside,
Her life had many a hope and aim,
Duties enough and little cares,
And now was quiet, now astir,
Till God's hand beckoned unawares—
And the sweet white brow is all of her.

III.
Is it too late then, Evelyn Hope?
What, your soul was pure and true,
The good stars met in your horoscope,
Made you of spirit, fire and dew—
And, just because I was thrice as old
And our paths in the world diverged so wide,
Each was nought to each, must I be told?
We were fellow mortals, nought beside?

IV.
No, indeed! for God above
Is great to grant, as mighty to make,
And creates the love to reward the love:
I claim you still, for my own love's sake!
Delayed it may be for more lives yet,
Through worlds I shall traverse, not a few:
Much is to learn, much to forget
Ere the time be come for taking you.

V.
But the time will come—at last it will,
When, Evelyn Hope, what meant (I shall say)
In the lower earth, in the years long still,
That body and soul so pure and gay?
Why your hair was amber, I shall divine,
And your mouth of your own geranium's red—
And what you would do with me, in fine,
In the new life come in the old one's stead.

VI.
I have lived (I shall say) so much since then,
Given up myself so many times,
Gained me the gains of various men,
Ransacked the ages, spoiled the climes;
Yet one thing, one, in my soul's full scope,
Either I missed or itself missed me:
And I want and find you, Evelyn Hope!
What is the issue? let us see!

VII.
I loved you, Evelyn, all the while!
My heart seemed full as it could hold;
There was place and to spare for the frank young smile,
And the red young mouth, and the hair's young gold.
So, hush—I will give you this leaf to keep:
See, I shut it inside the sweet cold hand!
There, that is our secret: go to sleep!
You will wake, and remember, and understand.

Mary, Queen of Scots

Henry Glassford Bell

I looked far back into other years, and lo, in bright array
I saw, as in a dream, the form of ages passed away.
It was a stately convent with its old and lofty walls,
And gardens with their broad green walks, where soft the footstep falls;
And o'er the antique dial-stones the creeping shadow passed,
And all around the noonday sun a drowsy radiance cast.
No sound of busy life was heard, save from the cloisters dim,
The tinkling of the silver bell, or the sisters' holy hymn.
And there five noble maidens sat, beneath the orchard trees,
In that first budding spring of youth, when all its prospects please;
And little recked they, when they sang, or knelt at vesper prayers,
That Scotland knew no prouder names—held none more dear than theirs;
And little even the loveliest thought, before the Virgin's shrine,
Of royal blood and high descent from the ancient Stuart line;
Calmly her happy days flew on, uncounted in their flight,
And as they flew they left behind a long-continuing light. …
The scene was changed: it was an eve of raw and surly mood,
And in a turret chamber high of ancient Holyrood
Sat Mary, listening to the rain and sighing with the winds,
That seemed to suit the stormy state of men's uncertain minds.
The touch of care had blanched her cheek, her smile was sadder now,
The weight of royalty had pressed too heavy on her brow;
And traitors to her councils came, and rebels to the field;
The Stuart sceptre well she swayed, but the sword she could not wield.
She thought of all her blighted hopes, the dreams of youth's brief day,
And summoned Rizzio with his lute, and bade the minstrel play
The songs she loved in early years—the songs of gay Navarre,
The songs, perchance, that erst were sung by gallant Chattilor.
They half beguiled her of her cares, they soothed her into smiles,
They won her thoughts from bigot zeal and fierce domestic broils;
But hark, the tramp of armed men, the Douglas' battle cry!
They come! they come! and lo, the scowl of Ruthven's hollow eye!
The swords are drawn, the daggers gleam, the tears and words are vain—
The ruffian steel is in his heart, the faithful Rizzio's slain!
Then Mary Stuart dashed aside the tears that trickling fell:
"Now for my father's arm!" she cried. "My woman's heart farewell!"
The scene was changed: it was a lake, with one small lonely isle,
And there, within the prison walls of its baronial pile,
Stern men stood menacing their queen, till she should stoop to sign
The traitorous scroll that snatched the crown from her ancestral line;
"My lords, my lords," the captive said, "were I but once more free,
With ten good knights on yonder shore to aid my cause and me,
This parchment would I scatter wide to every breeze that blows,
And once more reign a Stuart queen o'er my remorseless foes!"
A red spot burned upon her cheek, streamed her rich tresses down,
She wrote the words, she stood erect, a queen without a crown! …
The scene was changed: beside the block a sullen headsman stood,
And gleamed the broad axe in his hand, that soon must drip with blood.
With slow and steady step there came a lady through the hall,
And breathless silence chained the lips and touched the hearts of all.
Rich were the sable robes she wore—her white veil round her fell,
And from her neck there hung the cross—the cross she loved do well.
I knew that queenly form again, though blighted was its bloom;
I saw that grief and decked it out—an offering for the tomb!
I knew that eye, though faint its light, that once so brightly shone;
I knew the voice, though feeble now, that thrilled with every tone;
I knew the ringlets, almost gray, once threads of living gold;
I knew that bounding grace of step, that symmetry of mould!
Even now I see her far away, in that calm convent aisle,
I hear her chant her vesper hymn, I mark her holy smile;
Even now I see her bursting forth upon the bridal morn,

A new star in the firmament, to light and glory born!
Alas, the change! She placed her foot upon a triple throne,
And on the scaffold now she stands—beside the block—alone!
The little dog that licks her hand, the last of all the crowd
Who sunned themselves beneath her glance, and round her footsteps bowed.
Her neck is bared—the blow is struck—the soul is passed away!
The bright—the beautiful—is now a bleeding piece of clay.
The dog is moaning piteously; and, as it gurgles o'er,
Laps the warm blood that tricking runs unheeded to the floor.
The blood of beauty, wealth, and power, the heart-blood of a queen,
The noblest of the Stuart race, the fairest earth has seen,
Lapped by a dog! Go, think of it in silence and alone;
Then weigh against a grain of sand the glories of a throne.

From *Lancelot and Elaine*

Alfred, Lord Tennyson

"O sweet father, tender and true,
Deny me not," she said—"ye never yet
Denied my fancies—this, however strange,
My latest. Lay the letter in my hand
A little ere I die, and close the hand
Upon it; I shall guard it even in death.
And when the heat is gone from out my heart,
Then take the little bed on which I died
For Lancelot's love, and deck it like the Queen's
For richness, and me also like the Queen
In all I have of rich, and lay me on it.
And let there be prepared a chariot-bier
To take me to the river, and a barge
Be ready on the river, clothed in black.
I go in state to court, to meet the Queen.
There surely I shall speak for mine own self,
And none of you can speak for me so well.
And therefore let our dumb old man alone
Go with me; he can steer and row, and he
Will guide me to that palace, to the doors."

She ceased. Her father promised; whereupon
She grew so cheerful that they deemed her death
Was rather in the fantasy than the blood.
But ten slow mornings past, and on the eleventh
Her father laid the letter in her hand,
And closed the hand upon it, and she died.
So that day there was dole in Astolat.

But when the next sun brake from underground,
Then, those two brethren slowly with bent brows
Accompanying, the sad chariot-bier
Past like a shadow through the field, that shone
Full-summer, to that stream whereon the barge,
Palled all its length in blackest samite, lay.
There sat the lifelong creature of the house,
Loyal, the dumb old servitor, on deck,
Winking his eyes, and twisted all his face.
So those two brethren from the chariot took
And on the black decks laid her in her bed,
Set in her hand a lily, o'er her hung
The silken case with braided blazonings,
And kissed her quiet brows, and saying to her,
"Sister, farewell forever," and again,
"Farewell, sweet sister," parted all in tears.
Then rose the dumb old servitor, and the dead,
Oared by the dumb, went upward with the flood—
In her right hand the lily, in her left
The letter—all her bright hair streaming down—
And all the coverlid was cloth of gold
Drawn to her waist, and she herself in white
All but her face, and that clear-featured face
Was lovely, for she did not seem as dead,
But fast asleep, and lay as though she smiled.

****

... and the barge,
On to the palace-doorway sliding, paused.
There two stood armed, and kept the door; to whom,
All up the marble stair, tier over tier,
Were added mouths that gaped, and eyes that asked,
"What is it?" but the oarsman's haggard face,
As hard and still as is the face that men
Shape to their fancy's eye from broken rocks
On some cliff-side, appalled them, and they said,
"He is enchanted, cannot speak—and she,
Look how she sleeps—the Fairy Queen, so fair!
Yea, but how pale! what are they? flesh and blood?
Or come to take the King to Fairyland?
For some do hold our Arthur cannot die,
But that he passes into Fairyland."

While thus they babbled of the King, the King
Came girt with knights. Then turned the tongueless man
From the half-face to the full eye, and rose
And pointed to the damsel and the doors.
So Arthur bade the meek Sir Percivale
And pure Sir Galahad to uplift the maid;
And reverently they bore her into hall.
Then came the fine Gawain and wondered at her,
And Lancelot later came and mused at her,
And last the Queen herself, and pitied her;
But Arthur spied the letter in her hand,
Stoopt, took, brake seal, and read it; this was all:
"Most noble lord, Sir Lancelot of the Lake,
I, sometime called the maid of Astolat,
Come, for you left me taking no farewell,
Hither, to take my last farewell of you.
I loved you, and my love had no return,
And therefore my true love has been my death.
And therefore to our Lady Guinevere,

And to all other ladies, I make moan:
Pray for my soul, and yield me burial.
Pray for my soul thou too, Sir Lancelot,
As thou art a knight peerless."

Thus he read;
And ever in the reading lords and dames
Wept, looking often from his face who read
To hers which lay so silent, and at times,
So touched were they, half-thinking that her lips,
Who had devised the letter, moved again.
Then freely spoke Sir Lancelot to them all:
"My lord liege Arthur, and all ye that hear,
Know that for this most gentle maiden's death
Right heavy am I; for good she was and true,
But loved me with a love beyond all love
In women, whomsoever I have known.
Yet to be loved makes not to love again;
Not at my years, however it hold in youth.
I swear by truth and knighthood that I gave
No cause, not willingly, for such a love.
To this I call my friends in testimony,
Her brethren, and her father, who himself
Besought me to be plain and blunt, and use,
To break her passion, some discourtesy
Against my nature; what I could, I did.
I left her and I bade her no farewell;
Though, had I dreamt the damsel would have died,
I might have put my wits to some rough use,
And helped her from herself."

Maidenhood

Henry Wadsworth Longfellow

Maiden! with the meek, brown eyes,
In whose orbs a shadow lies
Like the dusk in evening skies!

Thou whose locks outshine the sun,
Golden tresses, wreathed in one,
As the braided streamlets run!

Standing, with reluctant feet,
Where the brook and river meet,
Womanhood and childhood fleet!

Gazing, with a timid glance,
On the brooklet's swift advance,
On the river's broad expanse!
Deep and still, that gliding stream
Beautiful to thee must seem,
As the river of a dream.

Then why pause with indecision,
When bright angels in thy vision
Beckon thee to fields Elysian?

Seest thou shadows sailing by,
As the dove, with startled eye,
Sees the falcon's shadow fly?

Hearest thou voices on the shore,
That our ears perceive no more,
Deafened by the cataract's roar?

O, thou child of many prayers!
Life hath quicksands—Life hath snares
Care and age come unawares!

Like the swell of some sweet tune,
Morning rises into noon,
May glides onward into June.
Childhood is the bough, where slumbered
Birds and blossoms many-numbered;—
Age, that bough with snows encumbered.

Gather, then, each flower that grows,
When the young heart overflows,
To embalm that tent of snows.
Bear a lily in thy hand;
Gates of brass cannot withstand
One touch of that magic wand.
Bear through sorrow, wrong, and ruth,
In thy heart the dew of youth,
On thy lips the smile of truth!
O, that dew, like balm, shall steal
Into wounds that cannot heal,
Even as sleep our eyes doth seal;

And that smile, like sunshine, dart
Into many a sunless heart,
For a smile of God thou art.

Mars La Tour (The Maiden's Vow)

A Legend of 1870-1871
Stafford MacGregor

In the valley of Avranches, the vespers were ringing,
A lullaby soft at the close of the day,
The white fleecy clouds the sunset was tinging
With many hued lights fading swiftly away,
Oft darkening to purple, now brightening to crimson,
Here braiding the edges with bands of bright gold,
As though the Aurora would win from the ocean,
Once more the avow that at daylight was told,
And increase the deep love that was whispered at dawn,
By enriching in splendor her robe of the morn.

As peaceful and bright in the year's opening days,
As that sunset, O France! Was thy future portrayed,
Though dark as the thunder-fraught cloud of the night,
Was that future when rolled page by page to the light.

O! where are the legions that bled for thy fame,
In the glory of victory on Austerlitz plain?
'Tis Valhubert of Avranches who heads the death roll,
"Died as general for France," so reads the scroll
On the statue in marble which Avranches has reared,
And which from his boyhood a grandson revered.

Not the fairest of maidens was Reinette de Veer,
Graceful in form, but of features severe,
Though equal in gifts always nature had blent,
And wreathed round her lips the smile of a saint,
And now as she hastens last adieux to hear
From that Valhubert's grandson, a young grenadier,
And nears the old abbey's ruined ivy clad aisle,
Her face wears in sadness that saintlike smile,
As kneeling she prays to our lady above
To shield from war's dangers her country and love.

As the white maid of Avenel, who of yore would appear
When a breast free of guile to her shrine should draw near
So a mystic white vision in the moonlight did gleam,
And in accents melodious as murmuring stream
To Reinette gave response, "Thou art not alone,
At the altars of Munich, of Dresden, of Cologne,
Are Germany's daughters now breathing like prayer
For those who must shortly for battle prepare,
Imploring at foot of the glory girt throne
Protection for loved ones, for country, for home.

Alas! gentle maiden, as ten moons shall wane,
Each moon by ten thousand shall number the slain,
As the billows that surge in yon bay's wide expanse,
Their green graves shall rise o'er their birthland of France.
And the blood of her sons by their kindred shall flow,
And your Paris be wrapped in a mantle of woe,
Domremy shall mourn, Vancouleurs hear the wail
That is born on the wings of the death-laden gale,
And the ramparts of Orleans all powerless shall be
To arrest the inroad of that wide spreading sea.

To far Northern Cambray the war note soon speeds,
And Laon and proud Lille hear the clattering steeds,
Whose riders bear message of bloody fields lost,
And foretell the advance of that merciless host.
The echoes of Tinchebray ten leagues from your town
Shall fling back the notes of the conqueror's drum,
From the passes of Vosges to the channel's far shore
From the forest of Ardennes to the vine-bordered Loire,
Exulting and proud with victorious glance,
Black eagles shall wave o'er one-fifth of fair France.

The shrine of St. Genevieve desecrated shall be,
And palaces flame to the roofs' topmost tree,
The Seine shall run red to Mante's ancient town,
Whose hamlets shall blaze and rafters crash down,
As in ages of yore when Duke William's bold band
Brought sword, flame and famine to ravage the land,
And whose wraith might well rise to see Calais in flames,
Rouen surrendered, Paris enchained,
And Normandy's sons, forgetting their line,
Marched by thousands as captives away to the Rhine—

Ah! Maurice, Reine faltered as forward he sped,
Methought that a vision appeared from the dead,
And grimly foreshadowed destruction and shame
To the sons of our country, but if with the slain
'Tis thy fate to be numbered, hear but my vow,
Ne'er at the high altar the knee I will bow,
As bride to another, but weep thee till death,
Encircle my brow with a funereal wreath,
And to another my troth I will plight,
Or cease to forget the adieu of to-night.

The forest of Scissy shall start from their bed,
Those forests that now deep in ocean are hid,
And the floods that surge hoarse in yonder broad bay,
Shall cease to spread shoreward their murmuring lay,
And St. Michael's weird towers that loom through the mist
Shall quake to their basement and crumble to dust,
And—but derisive and sharp o'er the deep shadowed glade
The notes of departure a bugle now played,
Proclaiming the hour of their parting was near,
To young Maurice Valhubert and Reinette de Veer.

On Mars la Tour high shone the sun and flashed again the Prussian Guns,
That swiftly wheel across the plain to wake the echoes of Lorraine,
And when towards the waning light had ceased their vengeful roar,
The Prussian sentries pace the heights of conquered Mars la Tour,
And as the roll was called that night by Metz's watch fires glare,
No answer to the name was heard of Maurice Valhubert
For why? the grandsire's scroll so terse, spoke not of when to fly,
But only taught to Valhubert, the lesson how to die,
And though no tablet marks the Grave of that young Grenadier,
To love and country true, he died for France and Reine de Veer.

Scripture References in *Anne of Green Gables*

Chapter 2:	
... Matthew was left to do that which was harder for him than ***bearding a lion in its den*** *...*	Daniel 6:16-28
Chapter 3:	
He seldom smoked, for Marilla ***set her face against it*** *...*	Leviticus 20:3, Ezekiel 15:7
Chapter 4:	
"The world doesn't seem such a ***howling wilderness*** *as it did last night."*	Deuteronomy 32:10
Chapter 8:	
"It will be uphill work, I expect, for Mrs. Thomas often told me I was ***desperately wicked.****"*	Jeremiah 17:9
Chapter 14:	
"But I've ***put my hand to the plough, and I won't look back.****"*	Luke 9:62
Chapter 16:	
"It was like ***heaping coals of fire on my head.****"*	Proverbs 25:21-22, Romans 12:20
*"****The stars in their courses fight against me****, Marilla."*	Judges 5:20
Chapter 17:	
... a note, ***most fearfully and wonderfully*** *twisted and folded ...*	Psalm 139:14
Chapter 21:	
... Anne, who was not entirely guiltless of the ***wisdom of the serpent*** *...*	Matthew 10:16
Chapter 26:	
"My ***besetting sin*** *is imagining too much and forgetting my duties."* *"... even ministers are human and have their* ***besetting sins*** *..."*	Hebrews 12:1
Chapter 27:	
chapter title: ***Vanity and Vexation of Spirit***	Ecclesiastes 1:14
"... I really felt that I had tasted ***the bitterness of death*** *..."*	1 Samuel 15:32
Chapter 31:	
"... and now I'm ***rejoicing as a strong man to run a race*** *..."*	Psalm 19:5
Especially did the Queen's class ***gird up their loins*** *for the fray ...*	Job 38:3
"... all silver and shallow and ***vision of things not seen.****"*	Hebrews 11:1

Shakespearean References in *Anne of Green Gables*

Chapter 3:	
Finally Marilla stepped lamely into the breach	*Henry V,* Act III, Scene i, L. 1-34
Chapter 5:	
"... a rose by any other name would smell as sweet ..."	*Romeo and Juliet,* Act II, Scene ii, L. 38-48
Chapter 14:	
... the Madonna lilies in the garden sent out whiffs of perfume that entered in on viewless winds ...	*Measure for Measure,* Act III, Scene i, L. 124
... Mark Antony's oration over the dead body of Caesar in the most heart-stirring tones ...	*Julius Caesar,* Act III, Scene ii, L. 78-112
Chapter 20:	
"... and I heard him say 'sweets to the sweet.'"	*Hamlet,* Act V, Scene i, L. 266
Chapter 25:	
... but Anne was the bright particular star of the occasion ...	*All's Well That Ends Well,* Act I, Scene i, L. 97
Chapter 26:	
To Anne in particular things seemed fearfully flat, stale, and unprofitable ...	*Hamlet,* Act I, Scene ii, L. 133-134

Tests

Anne of Green Gables

Midterm Test - Chapters 1-19

Name: ______________________________ Date: ____________

Give the name of the person who is speaking for each quote.

1. "Only don't say I didn't warn you if he burns Green Gables down or puts strychnine in the well—" ______________________

2. "I'm not in the depths of despair this morning. I never can be in the morning." ____________

3. "My life is a perfect graveyard of buried hopes." ______________________

4. "I guess it doesn't matter what a person's name is as long as he behaves himself." ____________

5. "I've been thinking over the idea until I've got kind of used to it. It seems a sort of duty." ____________

6. "Oh, Miss—Marilla, how much you miss!" ____________

7. "You can shut me up in a dark, damp dungeon inhabited by snakes and toads and feed me only on bread and water and I shall not complain." ____________

8. "Well, they didn't pick you for your looks, that's sure and certain." ____________

9. "But don't be too hard on her, Marilla. Recollect she hasn't ever had anyone to teach her right." ____________

10. "When did you ever hear of me starving people into good behavior?" ____________

11. "I'll imagine that I like them." ____________

12. "I am well in body although considerably rumpled up in spirit, thank you, ma'am." ____________

13. "I have to furnish most of the imagination, but I'm well able to do that." ____________

14. "I never saw such an infatuated man. The more she talks and the odder the things she says, the more he's delighted evidently." ____________

15. "You'll feel remorse of conscience some day, I expect, for breaking it, Marilla, but I forgive you." ____________

16. "Marilla, that is the first compliment I have ever had in my life and you can't imagine what a strange feeling it gave me." ____________

17. "The iron has entered into my soul, Diana." ____________

18. "The stars in their courses fight against me, Marilla." ____________

19. "… you will cover my life with a dark cloud of woe." ____________

20. "Please see that it is buried with me, for I don't believe I'll live very long." ________________

21. "There is no scope for imagination in it at all. Mr. Phillips says I'm the worst dunce he ever saw at it." ________________

22. "She seems to have a skill and presence of mind perfectly wonderful in a child of her age."
____

23. "I cannot tie myself down to anything so unromantic as dish-washing at this thrilling moment."
____

24. "I've come to confess, if you please." ________________

25. "… You seem like an interesting lady, and you might even be a kindred spirit although you don't look very much like it." ________________

Circle the correct response.

1. Mrs. Lynde's opinion of the Cuthberts' adoption of a child is that the child will:
   a. add warmth to their home
   b. burn down Green Gables
   c. be too expensive
2. When Anne gets to Green Gables, she is plunged into the depths of despair because:
   a. the house is too small
   b. Marilla is scary looking
   c. the Cuthberts wanted a boy
3. Anne's buried hope in her graveyard of buried hopes is that:
   a. her hair will not always be red
   b. she will learn to read
   c. she will have a sister
4. Anne is concerned that Marilla misses so much in life because she:
   a. doesn't use her imagination
   b. stays at home too much
   c. is uneducated
5. Marilla first witnesses Anne's short temper when Anne yells at:
   a. Mr. Phillips
   b. Gilbert
   c. Mrs. Lynde
6. Mr. Phillips says that Anne is the worst dunce he ever saw at:
   a. geometry
   b. calculus
   c. algebra

7. Anne displeases Mrs. Barry by:

   a. keeping Diana out late
   b. getting Diana drunk
   c. being rude to Mrs. Lynde

8. Anne proves her worth to Mrs. Barry when she:

   a. makes straight A's
   b. cleans the house for Marilla
   c. saves Minnie May's life

9. Anne and Diana mistakenly leap into bed with:

   a. Mrs. Lynde
   b. Minnie May
   c. Miss Josephine Barry

10. Anne is disappointed that the dresses Marilla makes for her don't have:

    a. puffed sleeves
    b. ruffles
    c. gold buttons

11. Anne has to furnish most of the imagination for herself and:

    a. Matthew
    b. Marilla
    c. Diana

12. When Marilla tells Anne she can't go to the picnic, Anne tells Marilla she has broken her:

    a. spirit
    b. heart
    c. back

13. Prissy Andrews tells Anne she has a pretty:

    a. complexion
    b. nose
    c. face

14. Iron enters Anne's soul when her name is spelled without an *e* by:

    a. Gilbert
    b. Mrs. Lynde
    c. Mr. Phillips

15. When Anne is separated from Diana, she tells Marilla that she should be buried with:

    a. a lock of Diana's hair
    b. a dress with puffed sleeves
    c. her hair braided

Fill in the blank.

1. Avonlea is located in ______________________________ .
2. The relationship between Matthew and Marilla is ______________________.
3. Matthew is mortally afraid of __________________________ .
4. Anne thinks she might be able to get a ____________________ to marry her.
5. Anne's bedroom is located in the __________________ room.
6. ________________ first decides that the Cuthberts should keep Anne.
7. ________________ has the authority in Anne's raising.
8. Anne doesn't care about God because ____________________________.
9. Anne's chief shortcoming is __________________________ .
10. The one thing Anne could never endure in a bosom friend is _____________________ .
11. The serious disposition Marilla discovers about Anne is her ______________________ .
12. ________________ convinces Anne to apologize to Mrs. Lynde.
13. Anne's apology becomes a triumph because she turns it into a ___________________ .
14. The most exciting thing about the church picnic is ____________________.
15. Anne almost misses the picnic because Marilla thinks Anne took her _________________ ________________ .
16. Marilla's first mistake in accusing Anne is her mistrust of Anne even though Anne has never ________________ to her before.
17. Gilbert makes an enemy of Anne by calling her _______________________.
18. Marilla's pudding sauce is ruined because a _________________ drowns in it.
19. Anne meets her Waterloo in _________________________ .
20. Diana is forbidden to speak to Anne by ___________________________.

Match the correct character to his/her description.

_______ 1. Matthew and Marilla Cuthbert

_______ 2. Miss Josephine Barry

_______ 3. Cordelia

_______ 4. Minnie May

_______ 5. Mrs. Rachel Lynde

_______ 6. Gilbert Blythe

_______ 7. Katie Maurice and Violetta

_______ 8. Diana Barry

_______ 9. Mrs. Thomas

_______10. Mr. Phillips

a. Diana's aunt

b. the Cuthberts' nosy neighbor

c. Diana's little sister who gets croup

d. owners of Green Gables

e. Anne's schoolmate and academic rival

f. the scrubwoman who took Anne in when her parents died

g. Anne's bosom friend

h. Anne's preferred name

i. Anne's imaginary friends

j. the school teacher at Avonlea

Essay: Give good, complete answers to these questions, using full sentences and perfect punctuation.

1. Matthew quickly becomes convinced that he and Marilla should keep Anne. What are his reasons for this decision?

2. Marilla tells Matthew, "When I fail, it'll be time enough to put your oar in." What does this statement mean?

3. Anne "heaps coals of fire" on Mrs. Barry's head. What does it mean to heap coals of fire on someone's head?

Vocabulary: Supply the Mastery Word that makes the most sense in the sentence.
Make sure to use the correct form.

aesthetic	arduous	deft	deprecate
diligent	estrange	irreverent	ostentatious
penitent	resolute	staunch	sublime
superfluous	tempestuous	vivacious	

1. Though he may appear old, Frank hasn't lost any of the _________________(n.) of his youth.
2. Since she has proved herself such a _________________(adj.) worker, we should give her the job.
3. At Derby I was overwhelmed by a sea of ___________________________(adj.) hats.
4. The _________________(adj.) journey had left the travelers tired and sore.
5. Although his crimes were laid before him, he was not ___________________(adj.), but was instead _____________________(adj.) in the idea that he was innocent.
6. The tank __________________(adv.) maneuvered its way through the mine field.
7. When they found out the designer had decorated their entire house in plaid, the clients greatly doubted her __________________(adj.) sense.
8. Just give me the facts and leave all the _____________________(adj.) information out.
9. Marcy was given a green balloon instead of red, which everyone else had received. It was strange that instead of feeling special, she simply felt __________________(adj.) from her group.
10. He stared _____________________(adv.) at the price tag, not believing it a fair amount to ask.
11. The star exited the plane and was greeted by a ___________________(adj.) crowd.
12. In some places of worship it can be considered ____________________(adj.) not to remove your hat when you enter the building.
13. "The most __________________(adj.) act is to set another before you." - William Blake
14. It takes a __________________(adj.) friend to stand by you even when you are wrong.

Bonus:

1. The two children strolled ________________(adv.) down the street.
2. After overthrowing the cruel dictator, the people were thankful for their new _________________(adj.) leader.
3. The coach admired the player's ________________(n.) on the field.
4. The poor job you did on cleaning your room is simply _____________________(adj.).

Anne of Green Gables

Midterm Test Answer Key - Chapters 1-19

Name: ______________________________ Date: ____________

Give the name of the person who is speaking for each quote.

1. "Only don't say I didn't warn you if he burns Green Gables down or puts strychnine in the well—" Mrs. Rachel Lynde
2. "I'm not in the depths of despair this morning. I never can be in the morning." Anne
3. "My life is a perfect graveyard of buried hopes." Anne
4. "I guess it doesn't matter what a person's name is as long as he behaves himself." Marilla
5. "I've been thinking over the idea until I've got kind of used to it. It seems a sort of duty." Marilla
6. "Oh, Miss—Marilla, how much you miss!" Anne
7. "You can shut me up in a dark, damp dungeon inhabited by snakes and toads and feed me only on bread and water and I shall not complain." Anne
8. "Well, they didn't pick you for your looks, that's sure and certain." Mrs. Rachel Lynde
9. "But don't be too hard on her, Marilla. Recollect she hasn't ever had anyone to teach her right." Matthew
10. "When did you ever hear of me starving people into good behavior?" Marilla
11. "I'll imagine that I like them." Anne
12. "I am well in body although considerably rumpled up in spirit, thank you, ma'am." Anne
13. "I have to furnish most of the imagination, but I'm well able to do that." Anne
14. "I never saw such an infatuated man. The more she talks and the odder the things she says, the more he's delighted evidently." Marilla
15. "You'll feel remorse of conscience some day, I expect, for breaking it, Marilla, but I forgive you." Anne
16. "Marilla, that is the first compliment I have ever had in my life and you can't imagine what a strange feeling it gave me." Anne
17. "The iron has entered into my soul, Diana." Anne
18. "The stars in their courses fight against me, Marilla." Anne
19. "… you will cover my life with a dark cloud of woe." Anne

20. "Please see that it is buried with me, for I don't believe I'll live very long." Anne

21. "There is no scope for imagination in it at all. Mr. Phillips says I'm the worst dunce he ever saw at it." Anne

22. "She seems to have a skill and presence of mind perfectly wonderful in a child of her age." the doctor

23. "I cannot tie myself down to anything so unromantic as dish-washing at this thrilling moment." Anne

24. "I've come to confess, if you please." Anne

25. "... You seem like an interesting lady, and you might even be a kindred spirit although you don't look very much like it." Anne

Circle the correct response.

1. Mrs. Lynde's opinion of the Cuthberts' adoption of a child is that the child will:
   - **a.** add warmth to their home
   - (**b.**) burn down Green Gables
   - **c.** be too expensive

2. When Anne gets to Green Gables, she is plunged into the depths of despair because:
   - **a.** the house is too small
   - **b.** Marilla is scary looking
   - (**c.**) the Cuthberts wanted a boy

3. Anne's buried hope in her graveyard of buried hopes is that:
   - (**a.**) her hair will not always be red
   - **b.** she will learn to read
   - **c.** she will have a sister

4. Anne is concerned that Marilla misses so much in life because she:
   - (**a.**) doesn't use her imagination
   - **b.** stays at home too much
   - **c.** is uneducated

5. Marilla first witnesses Anne's short temper when Anne yells at:
   - **a.** Mr. Phillips
   - **b.** Gilbert
   - (**c.**) Mrs. Lynde

6. Mr. Phillips says that Anne is the worst dunce he ever saw at:
   - (**a.**) geometry
   - **b.** calculus
   - **c.** algebra

7. Anne displeases Mrs. Barry by:

   a. keeping Diana out late
   (**b.**) getting Diana drunk
   c. being rude to Mrs. Lynde

8. Anne proves her worth to Mrs. Barry when she:

   a. makes straight A's
   b. cleans the house for Marilla
   (**c.**) saves Minnie May's life

9. Anne and Diana mistakenly leap into bed with:

   a. Mrs. Lynde
   b. Minnie May
   (**c.**) Miss Josephine Barry

10. Anne is disappointed that the dresses Marilla makes for her don't have:

   (**a.**) puffed sleeves
   b. ruffles
   c. gold buttons

11. Anne has to furnish most of the imagination for herself and:

   a. Matthew
   b. Marilla
   (**c.**) Diana

12. When Marilla tells Anne she can't go to the picnic, Anne tells Marilla she has broken her:

   a. spirit
   (**b.**) heart
   c. back

13. Prissy Andrews tells Anne she has a pretty:

   a. complexion
   (**b.**) nose
   c. face

14. Iron enters Anne's soul when her name is spelled without an *e* by:

   a. Gilbert
   b. Mrs. Lynde
   (**c.**) Mr. Phillips

15. When Anne is separated from Diana, she tells Marilla that she should be buried with:

   (**a.**) a lock of Diana's hair
   b. a dress with puffed sleeves
   c. her hair braided

Fill in the blank.

1. Avonlea is located in ___Nova Scotia, Canada___ .
2. The relationship between Matthew and Marilla is ___brother and sister___.
3. Matthew is mortally afraid of ___women and girls___ .
4. Anne thinks she might be able to get a ___foreign missionary___ to marry her.
5. Anne's bedroom is located in the ___east gable___ room.
6. ___Matthew___ first decides that the Cuthberts should keep Anne.
7. ___Marilla___ has the authority in Anne's raising.
8. Anne doesn't care about God because ___he gave her red hair___.
9. Anne's chief shortcoming is ___daydreaming___ .
10. The one thing Anne could never endure in a bosom friend is ___red hair___ .
11. The serious disposition Marilla discovers about Anne is her ___bad temper___ .
12. ___Matthew___ convinces Anne to apologize to Mrs. Lynde.
13. Anne's apology becomes a triumph because she turns it into a ___performance___ .
14. The most exciting thing about the church picnic is ___ice cream___.
15. Anne almost misses the picnic because Marilla thinks Anne took her ___amethyst brooch___ .
16. Marilla's first mistake in accusing Anne is her mistrust of Anne even though Anne has never ___lied___ to her before.
17. Gilbert makes an enemy of Anne by calling her ___Carrots___.
18. Marilla's pudding sauce is ruined because a ___mouse___ drowns in it.
19. Anne meets her Waterloo in ___geometry___ .
20. Diana is forbidden to speak to Anne by ___Mrs. Barry___.

Match the correct character to his/her description.

Answer	Character		Description
d	1. Matthew and Marilla Cuthbert	**a.**	Diana's aunt
a	2. Miss Josephine Barry	**b.**	the Cuthberts' nosy neighbor
h	3. Cordelia	**c.**	Diana's little sister who gets croup
c	4. Minnie May	**d.**	owners of Green Gables
b	5. Mrs. Rachel Lynde	**e.**	Anne's schoolmate and academic rival
e	6. Gilbert Blythe	**f.**	the scrubwoman who took Anne in when her parents died
i	7. Katie Maurice and Violetta	**g.**	Anne's bosom friend
g	8. Diana Barry	**h.**	Anne's preferred name
f	9. Mrs. Thomas	**i.**	Anne's imaginary friends
j	10. Mr. Phillips	**j.**	the school teacher at Avonlea

Essay: Give good, complete answers to these questions, using full sentences and perfect punctuation.

1. Matthew quickly becomes convinced that he and Marilla should keep Anne. What are his reasons for this decision?

   Matthew is charmed with Anne. Her frankness and open-hearted way of dealing with him puts him at ease immediately. He comes to see that even though he and Marilla were planning to adopt a boy to help them on the farm, Anne needs them. She needs to be loved, and Matthew quickly comes to the realization that he and Marilla can make a difference in a child's life.

2. Marilla tells Matthew, "When I fail, it'll be time enough to put your oar in." What does this statement mean?

   The analogy here is of Matthew and Marilla in a boat. Marilla will steer and control the boat with her oar, but Matthew won't even have his oar in the water until given permission by Marilla. Anne is the boat being steered. Marilla is taking control of raising Anne; Matthew will only be allowed to interfere when Marilla needs his help and gives him permission.

3. Anne "heaps coals of fire" on Mrs. Barry's head. What does it mean to heap coals of fire on someone's head?

   If you are forgiving and consistently nice in the face of being mistreated by others, you prove yourself to be a person of moral strength and character. As Paul says in Romans 12:21, you are overcoming evil with good. Anne heaps coals of fire on Mrs. Barry's head by totally forgiving her, even though Mrs. Barry was unwilling to do the same for Anne when she accidentally got Diana drunk.

Vocabulary: Supply the Mastery Word that makes the most sense in the sentence.
Make sure to use the correct form.

aesthetic	arduous	deft	deprecate
diligent	estrange	irreverent	ostentatious
penitent	resolute	staunch	sublime
superfluous	tempestuous	vivacious	

1. Though he may appear old, Frank hasn't lost any of the vivacity (n.) of his youth.
2. Since she has proved herself such a diligent (adj.) worker, we should give her the job.
3. At Derby I was overwhelmed by a sea of ostentatious (adj.) hats.
4. The arduous (adj.) journey had left the travelers tired and sore.
5. Although his crimes were laid before him, he was not penitent (adj.), but was instead resolute (adj.) in the idea that he was innocent.
6. The tank deftly (adv.) maneuvered its way through the mine field.
7. When they found out the designer had decorated their entire house in plaid, the clients greatly doubted her aesthetic (adj.) sense.
8. Just give me the facts and leave all the superfluous (adj.) information out.
9. Marcy was given a green balloon instead of red, which everyone else had received. It was strange that instead of feeling special, she simply felt estranged (adj.) from her group.
10. He stared deprecatingly (adv.) at the price tag, not believing it a fair amount to ask.
11. The star exited the plane and was greeted by a tempestuous (adj.) crowd.
12. In some places of worship it can be considered irreverent (adj.) not to remove your hat when you enter the building.
13. "The most sublime (adj.) act is to set another before you." - William Blake
14. It takes a staunch (adj.) friend to stand by you even when you are wrong.

Bonus:

1. The two children strolled blithely (adv.) down the street.
2. After overthrowing the cruel dictator, the people were thankful for their new benevolent (adj.) leader.
3. The coach admired the player's tenacity (n.) on the field.
4. The poor job you did on cleaning your room is simply reprehensible (adj.).

Anne of Green Gables

Final Test - Chapters 20-38

Name: ____ Date: ______________

Give the name of the person who is speaking for each quote.

1. "I can't tell you the person's name because I have vowed never to let it cross my lips."

   ____

2. "What would you feel like if a white thing did snatch me up and carry me off?"

   ____

3. "Oh, no, it takes me to make such a mistake." ____________________
4. "I really don't see how I'm going to live through the two weeks before school begins, I'm so impatient to see her." __________________________
5. "The thought that it is all my own fault is what makes it so hard. If I could blame it on anybody I would feel so much better." ________________________________
6. "If I had been killed she would have had to carry a dark burden of remorse all her life."

   ____

7. "When she pronounces my name I feel instinctively that she's spelling it with an *e*."

   ____

8. "Don't be alarmed if you hear me groaning." ____________________
9. "I knew he was up to some foolishness."______________________
10. "We're going to keep them all sacredly and have them to read to our descendants."

    ____

11. "Anne's a great hand at explaining." __________________________
12. "Little things like that are of no importance now because I don't suppose I'll ever be able to go anywhere again. My career is closed." ______________________
13. "You don't think much about romance when you have just escaped from a watery grave."

    ____

14. "If I'd a child like Anne in the house all the time I'd be a better and happier woman."

    ____

15. "He takes them spells oftener than he used to and I'm anxious about him."

    ____

16. "I did make a mistake in judging Anne, but it weren't no wonder, for an odder, unexpecteder witch of a child there never was in this world, that's what." _____________________________

17. “Oh, you good old friends, I’m glad to see your honest face once more …”

____

18. “It does seem as if it was the end of everything, doesn’t it?” ____________________

19. “I’m just dazzled inside.” ________________________

20. “I’d rather make people cry than laugh.” ________________________

21. “Now, I call that a positive triumph.” ___________________________

22. “What a splendid chin he has! I never noticed it before.” _______________________

23. “That Anne-girl improves all the time.” _________________________

24. “It’s not the first time I’ve been glad. You do like to rub things in, Matthew Cuthbert.”

____

25. “Well, now, I’d rather have you than a dozen boys, Anne. Just mind you that—rather than a dozen boys.” _________________________________

26. “When you’ve seen that look as often as I have you’ll know what it means.”

____

27. “She’s good and kind and sweet—but it’s not her sorrow—she’s outside of it and she couldn’t come close enough to my heart to help me. It’s our sorrow—yours and mine.”

____

28. “I did use to think you were possessed.” ______________________

29. “Nothing could be worse than giving up Green Gables—nothing could hurt me more.”

____

30. “But I can’t let you sacrifice yourself so for me. It would be terrible.” ______________________

31. “I feel as if you’d give me new life.” ___________________________

Circle the correct response.

1. The person who would have to “carry a dark burden of remorse all her life” when Anne falls from the ridge-pole is:
   - **a.** Diana Barry
   - **b.** Josie Pye
   - **c.** Prissy Andrews
2. Anne feels that she will never be able to go anywhere again when she:
   - **a.** dyes her hair green
   - **b.** ruins a cake
   - **c.** falls from a ridge-pole

3. Anne almost drowns when pretending to be:

   a. Guinevere
   b. a damsel in distress
   c. Elaine, the Lady of Shalott

4. The good friends Anne is happy to see again after the summer are:

   a. her school books
   b. the Pyes
   c. Prissy and Jane

5. Who wins first place on the Queen's test?

   a. Anne
   b. Gilbert
   c. Anne and Gilbert

6. Anne would rather make people cry than laugh when she:

   a. sings
   b. recites
   c. dances

7. The person who pronounces Matthew dead is:

   a. Mrs. Lynde
   b. Marilla
   c. Anne

8. When Mrs. Allan comes to tea, Anne ruins a:

   a. pudding
   b. cake
   c. pie

9. Anne thinks that if she were invited to tea every day she would be:

   a. a model child
   b. happier
   c. very full

10. When Anne is injured, the wish that is granted to her is:

    a. her hair fades to auburn
    b. Miss Stacy visits her
    c. she faints

11. Marilla believes that Miss Stacy's concert is:

    a. a great idea
    b. foolishness and nonsense
    c. a good way to raise money

12. Anne thinks the most romantic ending to a story is a:

    a. wedding
    b. feast
    c. funeral

13. To get rid of red hair, Anne was willing to risk:

    a. being a little wicked
    b. missing school
    c. not doing her homework

14. When Gilbert first seeks to make peace with Anne, she:

    a. rejects him
    b. kisses him
    c. ignores him

15. Moody Spurgeon steadies his nerves by:

    a. praying
    b. eating
    c. reciting the multiplication tables

16. Anne's refusal to fail in front of Gilbert helps her to overcome:

    a. her failure at geometry
    b. her stage fright
    c. her shyness

17. Matthew's death is precipitated by:

    a. ruined crops
    b. failure of the bank
    c. disappointment in Anne

18. Anne saves Green Gables by:

    a. selling her possessions
    b. marrying Gilbert
    c. giving up her college scholarship

Fill in the blank.

1. Anne could never be a minister's wife because she is not ____________________.
2. When Anne falls from the ridge-pole, she breaks her ________________________.
3. When Anne is injured, Marilla realizes that Anne is ____________________ to her.
4. Matthew gives Anne ___________________________ for Christmas.
5. Aunt Josephine gives Anne ________________________________ for Christmas.
6. Anne's besetting sin is ________________________ .
7. Diana ends her stories by _________________________________ .
8. Anne is rescued from a watery grave by ____________________ .
9. The best part of Anne's trip to the city to visit Aunt Josephine is ________________________ .
10. ____________________ is convinced that Anne will excel on the Queen's test before she even takes it.
11. Anne is given a string of pearl beads by ____________________ .
12. The Queen's medal is won by __________________, and the Avery scholarship is won by __________________ .
13. Gilbert gives up the school teaching job in ____________________ in order to help Anne.
14. At the end of the book, Anne ________________________ Gilbert.
15. Anne's bend in the road is _______________________________ .

Match the correct character to his/her description.

_______ 1. the Sunday School Superintendent

_______ 2. Anne's friend who is going to be a minister

_______ 3. Anne's favorite minister

_______ 4. Anne's inspiring teacher

_______ 5. Anne's beloved minster's wife

_______ 6. Anne's friend who always insults her

Essay: Give good, complete answers to these questions, using full sentences and perfect punctuation.

1. Describe Anne's relationship with Matthew. How does it differ from her relationship with Marilla?

2. How does Matthew credit Providence with the mistake that resulted in Anne coming to live at Green Gables?

3. When Anne feels guilty for beginning to take joy in life again after Matthew's death, how does Mrs. Allan comfort her?

Vocabulary: Supply the Mastery Word that makes the most sense in the sentence.
Make sure to use the correct form. *Not every word will be used.

aesthetic	arduous	chasten	deft
deprecate	diligent	eclipse	estrange
evince	implicit	inert	infatuated
inscrutable	irreverent	ostentatious	penitent
pithy	precarious	propitious (un-)	prosaic
provincial	quaint	resolute	staunch
sublime	superfluous	succumb	tempestuous
veracity/ veracious	vivacious		

1. The book of Proverbs is full of ________________(adj.) sayings that ________________________(v.) the wisdom of Solomon.
2. The captain refused to ____________________(v.) to the taunts of the enemy.
3. Amanda was __________________(adj.) during her speech, winning the crowd as if she were acting out a play. Scott, however, was ___________________(adj.) and not compelling.
4. Ajax was angry that Odysseus' fame ____________________(v.) his own.
5. The possibility of finally beating their biggest rivals was a _________________(v.) thought.
6. Losing the paddle in the middle of the lake has put us in a ______________________(adj.) position.
7. His older brother always tried to ___________________(v.) Mark's pride by beating him at everything.
8. No matter how _____________________(adj.) the homework, Freddie always worked _______________________(adv.) and completed it.
9. The police questioned all the witnesses to ensure the ___________________(n.) of the story.
10. Despite his many injuries, he thought the fall was ______________________(adj.), considering the fact that he survived.
11. The ___________________(adj.) thief sought to restore all he had stolen.
12. Although the boy grew up in a small, __________________(adj.) town, he learned valuable lessons there that would later benefit him in the world of business.
13. "This world, after all our science and sciences, is still a miracle; wonderful, __________________(adj.), magical, and more, to whosoever will think of it." - Thomas Dekker
14. To the disciples' amazement, Jesus was able to calm the ______________________(adj.) sea.
15. David hurled the stone _________________(adv.) at the giant's head.

16. Paris was ______________________(v.) from the first moment he laid eyes on Helen.

17. The television is powerful enough to turn even the most active youth into an __________________(adj.) blob for hours at a time.

18. "The erection of a monument is _______________________(adj.); our memory will endure if our lives have deserved." - Pliny the Younger

19. A child's love for his parents may be _______________________(adj.), but it doesn't mean he shouldn't tell them often.

20. You don't have to change the structure of the house, just make some additions so that it is more _______________________(adv.) pleasing.

21. The man started waving ____________________(adv.) when his ride started to pull away without him.

22. The young couple's first house certainly wasn't grand, but it was delightfully ___________________(adj.).

Bonus:

1. The girl ____________________(v.) her brother to give her back the doll.
2. When the lake is ____________________(adj.) it looks like a giant sheet of glass.
3. Marcy was quite _____________________(adj.) about the thin rope that was supposed to support her high in the air.
4. She was a _____________________(adj.) supporter of the arts, never failing to give of her time and money.
5. The _________________________(adj.) man had, out of nowhere, found a guitar and started singing to the people waiting in line for the movie.

Anne of Green Gables

Final Test Answer Key - Chapters 20-38

Name: ______________________________ Date: ____________

Give the name of the person who is speaking for each quote.

1. "I can't tell you the person's name because I have vowed never to let it cross my lips." Anne
2. "What would you feel like if a white thing did snatch me up and carry me off?" Anne
3. "Oh, no, it takes me to make such a mistake." Anne
4. "I really don't see how I'm going to live through the two weeks before school begins, I'm so impatient to see her." Anne
5. "The thought that it is all my own fault is what makes it so hard. If I could blame it on anybody I would feel so much better." Anne
6. "If I had been killed she would have had to carry a dark burden of remorse all her life." Anne
7. "When she pronounces my name I feel instinctively that she's spelling it with an *e*." Anne
8. "Don't be alarmed if you hear me groaning." Anne
9. "I knew he was up to some foolishness." Marilla
10. "We're going to keep them all sacredly and have them to read to our descendants." Anne
11. "Anne's a great hand at explaining." Matthew
12. "Little things like that are of no importance now because I don't suppose I'll ever be able to go anywhere again. My career is closed." Anne
13. "You don't think much about romance when you have just escaped from a watery grave." Anne
14. "If I'd a child like Anne in the house all the time I'd be a better and happier woman." Miss Josephine Barry
15. "He takes them spells oftener than he used to and I'm anxious about him." Marilla
16. "I did make a mistake in judging Anne, but it weren't no wonder, for an odder, unexpecteder witch of a child there never was in this world, that's what." Mrs. Rachel Lynde

17. "Oh, you good old friends, I'm glad to see your honest face once more ..."
Anne

18. "It does seem as if it was the end of everything, doesn't it?" Diana

19. "I'm just dazzled inside." Anne

20. "I'd rather make people cry than laugh." Anne

21. "Now, I call that a positive triumph." Anne

22. "What a splendid chin he has! I never noticed it before." Anne

23. "That Anne-girl improves all the time." Miss Josephine Barry

24. "It's not the first time I've been glad. You do like to rub things in, Matthew Cuthbert."
Marilla

25. "Well, now, I'd rather have you than a dozen boys, Anne. Just mind you that—rather than a dozen boys." Matthew

26. "When you've seen that look as often as I have you'll know what it means."
Mrs. Rachel Lynde

27. "She's good and kind and sweet—but it's not her sorrow—she's outside of it and she couldn't come close enough to my heart to help me. It's our sorrow—yours and mine."
Anne

28. "I did use to think you were possessed." Marilla

29. "Nothing could be worse than giving up Green Gables—nothing could hurt me more."
Anne

30. "But I can't let you sacrifice yourself so for me. It would be terrible." Marilla

31. "I feel as if you'd give me new life." Marilla

Circle the correct response.

1. The person who would have to "carry a dark burden of remorse all her life" when Anne falls from the ridge-pole is:
   - **a.** Diana Barry
   - **(b.)** Josie Pye
   - **c.** Prissy Andrews

2. Anne feels that she will never be able to go anywhere again when she:
   - **(a.)** dyes her hair green
   - **b.** ruins a cake
   - **c.** falls from a ridge-pole

3. Anne almost drowns when pretending to be:

   a. Guinevere
   b. a damsel in distress
   (c.) Elaine, the Lady of Shalott

4. The good friends Anne is happy to see again after the summer are:

   (a.) her school books
   b. the Pyes
   c. Prissy and Jane

5. Who wins first place on the Queen's test?

   a. Anne
   b. Gilbert
   (c.) Anne and Gilbert

6. Anne would rather make people cry than laugh when she:

   a. sings
   (b.) recites
   c. dances

7. The person who pronounces Matthew dead is:

   (a.) Mrs. Lynde
   b. Marilla
   c. Anne

8. When Mrs. Allan comes to tea, Anne ruins a:

   a. pudding
   (b.) cake
   c. pie

9. Anne thinks that if she were invited to tea every day she would be:

   (a.) a model child
   b. happier
   c. very full

10. When Anne is injured, the wish that is granted to her is:

   a. her hair fades to auburn
   b. Miss Stacy visits her
   (c.) she faints

11. Marilla believes that Miss Stacy's concert is:

   a. a great idea
   (b.) foolishness and nonsense
   c. a good way to raise money

12. Anne thinks the most romantic ending to a story is a:

   a. wedding
   b. feast
   (c.) funeral

13. To get rid of red hair, Anne was willing to risk:

   (a.) being a little wicked
   b. missing school
   c. not doing her homework

14. When Gilbert first seeks to make peace with Anne, she:

   (a.) rejects him
   b. kisses him
   c. ignores him

15. Moody Spurgeon steadies his nerves by:

   a. praying
   b. eating
   (c.) reciting the multiplication tables

16. Anne's refusal to fail in front of Gilbert helps her to overcome:

   a. her failure at geometry
   (b.) her stage fright
   c. her shyness

17. Matthew's death is precipitated by:

   a. ruined crops
   (b.) failure of the bank
   c. disappointment in Anne

18. Anne saves Green Gables by:

   a. selling her possessions
   b. marrying Gilbert
   (c.) giving up her college scholarship

Fill in the blank.

1. Anne could never be a minister's wife because she is not naturally good.
2. When Anne falls from the ridge-pole, she breaks her ankle.
3. When Anne is injured, Marilla realizes that Anne is dear to her.
4. Matthew gives Anne a dress with puffed sleeves for Christmas.
5. Aunt Josephine gives Anne kid slippers for Christmas.
6. Anne's besetting sin is daydreaming.
7. Diana ends her stories by killing everyone off.
8. Anne is rescued from a watery grave by Gilbert.
9. The best part of Anne's trip to the city to visit Aunt Josephine is coming home.
10. Matthew is convinced that Anne will excel on the Queen's test before she even takes it.
11. Anne is given a string of pearl beads by Matthew.
12. The Queen's medal is won by Gilbert, and the Avery scholarship is won by Anne.
13. Gilbert gives up the school teaching job in Avonlea in order to help Anne.
14. At the end of the book, Anne forgives Gilbert.
15. Anne's bend in the road is the death of Matthew.

Match the correct character to his/her description.

c 1. the Sunday School Superintendent
f 2. Anne's friend who is going to be a minister
b 3. Anne's favorite minister
e 4. Anne's inspiring teacher
a 5. Anne's beloved minster's wife
d 6. Anne's friend who always insults her

a. Mrs. Allan
b. Mr. Allan
c. Mr. Bell
d. Josie Pye
e. Miss Stacy
f. Moody Spurgeon

Essay: Give good, complete answers to these questions, using full sentences and perfect punctuation.

1. Describe Anne's relationship with Matthew. How does it differ from her relationship with Marilla?

Matthew falls in love with Anne almost immediately. He is delighted with her conversation and appreciation for the world. He is fully confident that she will excel in whatever she attempts and lavishes praise on her when she does succeed. He is a ready listener and always gives her the benefit of the doubt. He is openly affectionate and loving to Anne. Marilla doesn't often tell Anne how much she loves her. And since Marilla has the responsibility of raising Anne, it falls on her to be the rule-maker and disciplinarian.

2. How does Matthew credit Providence with the mistake that resulted in Anne coming to live at Green Gables?

Matthew originally decides that he and Marilla should adopt Anne because she needs them. But, ultimately, he comes to the conclusion that God brought Anne to them because they needed her in their lives. He is thankful for God blessing them with Anne's presence.

3. When Anne feels guilty for beginning to take joy in life again after Matthew's death, how does Mrs. Allan comfort her?

Mrs. Allan tells Anne that Matthew liked to hear her laugh and to know that she took pleasure in the world around her. Even though he is no longer on earth, Matthew would still want to know that Anne had not lost her joy in life. He would want her to move beyond her grief and begin living fully again.

Vocabulary: Supply the Mastery Word that makes the most sense in the sentence.
Make sure to use the correct form. *Not every word will be used.

aesthetic	arduous	chasten	deft
deprecate	diligent	eclipse	estrange
evince	implicit	inert	infatuated
inscrutable	irreverent	ostentatious	penitent
pithy	precarious	propitious (un-)	prosaic
provincial	quaint	resolute	staunch
sublime	superfluous	succumb	tempestuous
veracity/ veracious	vivacious		

1. The book of Proverbs is full of ____pithy____(adj.) sayings that ____evince____(v.) the wisdom of Solomon.
2. The captain refused to ____succumb____(v.) to the taunts of the enemy.
3. Amanda was ____vivacious____(adj.) during her speech, winning the crowd as if she were acting out a play. Scott, however, was ____prosaic____(adj.) and not compelling.
4. Ajax was angry that Odysseus' fame ____eclipsed____(v.) his own.
5. The possibility of finally beating their biggest rivals was a ____sublime____(v.) thought.
6. Losing the paddle in the middle of the lake has put us in a ____precarious____(adj.) position.
7. His older brother always tried to ____chasten____(v.) Mark's pride by beating him at everything.
8. No matter how ____arduous____(adj.) the homework, Freddie always worked ____diligently____(adv.) and completed it.
9. The police questioned all the witnesses to ensure the ____veracity____(n.) of the story.
10. Despite his many injuries, he thought the fall was ____propitious____(adj.), considering the fact that he survived.
11. The ____penitent____(adj.) thief sought to restore all he had stolen.
12. Although the boy grew up in a small, ____provincial____(adj.) town, he learned valuable lessons there that would later benefit him in the world of business.
13. "This world, after all our science and sciences, is still a miracle; wonderful, ____inscrutable____(adj.), magical, and more, to whosoever will think of it." - Thomas Dekker
14. To the disciples' amazement, Jesus was able to calm the ____tempestuous____(adj.) sea.
15. David hurled the stone ____deftly____(adv.) at the giant's head.

16. Paris was infatuated (v.) from the first moment he laid eyes on Helen.

17. The television is powerful enough to turn even the most active youth into an inert (adj.) blob for hours at a time.

18. "The erection of a monument is superfluous (adj.); our memory will endure if our lives have deserved." - Pliny the Younger

19. A child's love for his parents may be implicit (adj.), but it doesn't mean he shouldn't tell them often.

20. You don't have to change the structure of the house, just make some additions so that it is more aesthetically (adv.) pleasing.

21. The man started waving ostentatiously (adv.) when his ride started to pull away without him.

22. The young couple's first house certainly wasn't grand, but it was delightfully quaint (adj.).

Bonus:

1. The girl entreated (v.) her brother to give her back the doll.
2. When the lake is tranquil (adj.) it looks like a giant sheet of glass.
3. Marcy was quite skeptical (adj.) about the thin rope that was supposed to support her high in the air.
4. She was a staunch/benevolent (adj.) supporter of the arts, never failing to give of her time and money.
5. The capricious (adj.) man had, out of nowhere, found a guitar and started singing to the people waiting in line for the movie.